BODLEIANALIA

BODLEIANALIA

Curious Facts about Britain's
Oldest University Library

CLAIRE COCK-STARKEY
& VIOLET MOLLER

Bodleian Library
UNIVERSITY OF OXFORD

First published in 2016 by the Bodleian Library
Broad Street, Oxford OX1 3BG

www.bodleianshop.co.uk

ISBN 978 1 85124 252 8

Text © Bodleian Library, University of Oxford, 2016

Cover design by Dot Little at the Bodleian Library
Designed and typeset by illuminati in Monotype Joanna
Printed and bound in Great Britain by TJ International Ltd, Padstow,
Cornwall, on 80 gsm Munken Premium cream paper

British Library Catalogue in Publishing Data
A CIP record of this publication is available from the British Library

INTRODUCTION

The earliest incarnation of a University library in Oxford was a trunk of items kept in a room over the Congregation House next to St Mary's Church. In 1439 and 1444 Humfrey, Duke of Gloucester (brother of Henry V), gave to the University a major part of his personal library of over 260 books, which was housed in a splendid purpose-built room above the Divinity School. Refounded by Thomas Bodley in 1602, the library has grown enormously over the course of its 400-year history. Today Bodleian Libraries encompasses thirty dependent libraries and has become the largest academic library system in Europe. The Bodleian is also the oldest university library in the UK and the second largest library in the country.

The Bodleian now holds some 12 million items, offers a huge variety of special collections material, from music-hall ephemera to Sanskrit manuscripts, and boasts a very wide array of treasures, including a Gutenberg Bible and five original (thirteenth-century) copies of Magna Carta. In 1605 Francis Bacon wrote to Sir Thomas Bodley that in founding his library at Oxford he had 'built an Ark to save learning from deluge'. In this book, highlights from that Ark have been distilled down to the most intriguing and interesting facts.

Inevitably, in such a complex institution, there is some debate over the exact dates or details of events, and several of these are now hidden by time. For the same reason it is sometimes difficult to obtain a consensus on what is the oldest or most valuable item in a library with such a long history.

Drawing on such rich material, it has proved impossible to include every anecdote and treasure of note, but we hope *Bodleianalia* gives a flavour of the Bodleian Library and encourages the reader to explore its history further.

Bodleianalia owes a huge debt to Mary Clapinson's *A Brief History of the Bodleian Library*, Geoffrey Tyack's *Bodleian Library: Souvenir Guide*, Stephen Hebron's *Dr Radcliffe's Library* and David Vaisey's *Bodleian Library Treasures*. Additionally many thanks must go to Dr Frankie Wilson, Head of Assessment at Bodleian Libraries, for providing and explaining recent statistics about the Library; to Virginia Lladó-Buisán, Head of Conservation and Collection Care, and her team, for their help explaining fasiculing and book conservation; to Sarah Wheale, Head of Rare Books, for her invaluable information on shelfmarks, book classification and catalogues; and to Bruce Barker-Benfield, John Duffy, Clive Hurst and curatorial staff for checking sections of the material.

DUKE HUMFREY'S LIBRARY,
ARTS END & SELDEN END

Duke Humfrey (1390–1447) was Duke of Gloucester and youngest brother of Henry V. He was a keen collector of manuscripts. In 1439 he gifted 129 manuscripts to Oxford University and in 1444 a further 134 items. This sudden influx swamped the existing small library housed in the Congregation House of the University Church of St Mary the Virgin, and a new library building was deemed necessary. In 1444 it was agreed that Duke Humfrey's Library would be built above the Divinity School. Until recently Duke Humfrey's was the reading room for manuscripts and rare books (now read in the Weston Library); today it operates as a reading room for higher-level studies in the Humanities. A timeline of some of the major events in the history of Duke Humfrey's Library is given below:

1478	Building commenced
1488	Building completed
1550	Library closed during English Reformation after it is stripped of books*
1598	Thomas Bodley refurbished the library
1602	Library reopened
1612	Arts End completed
1640	Selden End completed
1756	Old benches between bookshelves replaced with 36 Windsor chairs†

* During the Reformation Edward VI ordered that Roman Catholic books be purged from the Library. The historian Anthony Wood described the dispersal of books thus: 'some of those books so taken out by the Reformers were burnt, some sold away for Robin Hood's pennyworths, either to Booksellers, or to Glovers to press their gloves, or Taylors to make measures, or to Bookbinders to cover books bound by them, and some also kept by the Reformers for their own use.'

† The library was originally furnished with wooden lecterns, 1.7 metres high, at which scholars could stand and study the manuscripts, which would have been chained to the lectern. By 1556 these lecterns had been sold; however, during the refurbishment of the library in the 1960s the outlines of the medieval lecterns, which had been hidden by book presses, were uncovered.

1757	Chains securing books to the shelves removed*
1845	Steam heating introduced
1876	Lead roof replaced with copper
1926	Rotten ceiling repaired
1929	Electric lighting installed
1953	New heating system installed
1963	Reopened as a reading room after restoration
1979	Closed to the general public
1980s	Guided tours of the library began
1998	Death-watch beetle infestation in roof timbers sparked refurbishment

In 1608 Thomas Bodley decided the existing library needed to be extended and sourced some free wood for the building from the king's woods in Shotover and Stow. Additionally, Francis, Lord Norris donated twenty oak trees from his estate in Rycote. Originally Duke Humfrey's Library contained books for the 'higher faculties', which were theology, law and medicine. Everything else was classified as 'arts' and so was shelved in this new building, now dubbed Arts End. Arts End was completed in 1612 and was the first of a new type of library building in England, with the walls shelved from floor to ceiling and a gallery giving access to the upper floor.

As the collection grew, so too did the library building. In 1634–37 Selden End (though it was not so named at the time it was built) was built as a further extension to Duke Humfrey's Library and ended up housing the 8,000 books gifted to the library by Lawyer John Selden (1584–1654): it was thus named in his honour. The original locked cases with ornamental grilles to hold valuable manuscripts in the Selden End survive to this day. The whole complex of Selden End, Duke Humfrey's and Arts End are in the shape of the letter 'H', a design conceived by Bodley himself.

---

* Nathaniel Bull, a blacksmith, unchained 1,448 volumes between 1760 and 1761 and for this was paid £3 0s 4d.

PRIME MINISTERS' PAPERS

The Bodleian holds the papers of seven former British prime ministers (terms of office in parentheses):

H.H. Asquith (1908–16)
Clement Attlee (1945–51)
James Callaghan (1976–79)
Benjamin Disraeli (1868, 1874–80)
Edward Heath (1970–74)
Harold Macmillan (1957–63)
Harold Wilson (1964–70, 1974–76)

THE HIGHWAYMAN AND THE LIBRARY

In 1720 highwayman John Hawkins came to Oxford and visited the Bodleian. His accomplice Ralph Wilson wrote an account of their many criminal exploits and recorded this of their trip to Oxford:

In the mean time, Jack Hawkins and I were consulting where to conceal ourselves; at last we pitch'd upon Oxford, whither we walk'd a foot, and tarried there a Month: in which time nothing remarkable happen'd, except that Hawkins defaced some Pictures in the Gallery above the Bodleian Library, for the Discovery whereof the University bid 100 l. A poor Taylor, who had above measure distinguish'd himself for a Whig, was taken up and imprisoned for this Fact, and very narrowly escaped a whipping.

Given the spree of robbery and destruction in the early 1720s that Hawkins took part in, the Library got off lightly. Hawkins was eventually hanged at Tyburn on 21 May 1722 for robbing hundreds of people.

BODLEY'S LIBRARIANS

To date there have been twenty-five Bodley's Librarians:

1st	1600–20	Thomas James
2nd	1620–52	John Rouse
3rd	1652–60	Thomas Barlow
4th	1660–65	Thomas Lockey
5th	1665–1701	Thomas Hyde
6th	1701–19	John Hudson
7th	1719–29	Joseph Bowles
8th	1729–47	Robert Fysher
9th	1747–68	Humphrey Owen
10th	1768–1813	John Price
11th	1813–60	Bulkeley Bandinel
12th	1860–82	Henry Octavius Coxe
13th	1882–1912	Edward Williams Byron Nicholson
14th	1912–19	Falconer Madan
15th	1919–31	Sir Arthur Ernest Cowley
16th	1931–45	Sir (Henry Herbert) Edmund Craster
17th	1945–48	H.R. Creswick
18th	1948–66	(John) Nowell Linton Myres
19th	1966–79	Robert Shackleton
20th	1979–82	(Erik) Richard (Sidney) Fifoot
21st	1982–86	John W. Jolliffe
22nd	1986–97	David G. Vaisey
23rd	1997–2007	Reg P. Carr
24th	2007–14	Sarah E. Thomas
25th	2014–	Richard Ovenden

A MEMORIAL CONCERNING THE
STATE OF THE BODLEIAN LIBRARY

In 1787 Thomas Beddoes, a reader in Chemistry and member
of Pembroke College, issued a pamphlet critical of the way
in which the Bodleian Library was, at that time, run. The
pamphlet was addressed to the Library's governing body of
curators and was titled *A Memorial Concerning the State of the Bodleian Library, and the Conduct of the Principal Librarian*. In it Beddoes
listed a number of issues he had with the Library, including
the limited opening hours (see p. 44), poor selection of new
books and lack of foreign publications, but he reserved his
most fervent ire for John Price, the tenth Bodley's Librarian:

> The first clause of the statute ... enjoins that the Librarian
> be not encumbered with a *beneficium curatum* [a church
> office with pay] ... and in the same paragraph he is
> required to be at hand every day, or, as it is expressed
> with greater laxity in the *Reliquiae Bodleianae* 'almost every
> day'.
>
> The present Librarian is known to have lived in open
> defiance of this regulation. At the time when he became
> a candidate for the office, he was said to have thought it
> necessary to resign his living; though it is evident, that
> the very same thing which disqualified him for receiving
> his office, must disqualify him for retaining it.
>
> He likewise serves a curacy at about 11 miles distance
> from the University, which occupation occasions a regu-
> lar and constant neglect of his duty. If I had not myself
> so often experienced the inconveniences arising from
> his absence, I should have been content to wonder, with
> others, at the toleration of this open and deliberate vio-
> lation of the statute. But it unfortunately happens, from
> the disposition of the Chemical Lectures, that I have
> scarce any leisure, but on Saturdays and Mondays, to
> consult such books as may assist me in preparing them.
> Accordingly, on those days I have frequently resorted

to the library, and have been uniformly disappointed, because the Librarian alone could supply me with what I wanted. On expressing my surprise that he should be so often absent, I was told by the Under-librarians, that he was gone to his curacy; which, as I learned, from farther enquiry, commonly detains him from Oxford both those days.

There is no record of John Price making any reply to the accusations levelled at him, and indeed he carried on in his post until his death in 1813. The pamphlet did have some effect though, as the curators increased staffing levels to ensure that the Library was opened at the appointed times, which may have gone some way to mollifying Beddoes.

THE BODLEIAN OATH

All readers admitted to use the Bodleian must take an oath. Sir Thomas Bodley's original 'oath of fidelity' was as follows:

> You shall promise and swear in the presence of al-
> mightie God, that whensoever you shall repaire to the
> publique Librarie of this Universitie, you will conforme
> to your self to studie with modestie and silence, and
> use both the bookes and everything els appertaining
> to their furniture, with a careful respect to their long-
> est conservation; and that neither your self in person,
> nor any other whosoever, by your procurement or
> privitie, shall either openly or underhand, by way of
> embezeling, changing, razing, defacing, tearing, cut-
> ting, noting, interlining, or by voluntarie corrupting,
> blotting, slurring or any other maner of mangling, or
> misusing, any one or more of the saied bookes, either
> wholly or in part, make any alteration: but shall hinder
> and impeache, so much as lieth in yow, all and every
> offendour or offendours, by detecting their demeanour

unto the Vice-chancellour, or to his Deputie then in place, within the next three daies after it shall com to your knowledge, so helpe you God by Christian merites, according to the doctrine of his holy Evengelistes.

Since 1970 the oath has been somewhat refined and is now the rather more snappy:

I hereby undertake not to remove from the Library, or to mark, deface, or injure in any way, any volume, document, or other object belonging to it, or in its custody; not to bring into the Library or kindle therein any fire or flame, and not to smoke in the Library; and I promise to obey all rules of the Library.

In 1980 Mgr José Ruysschaert, the vice prefect of manuscripts at the Vatican Library, applied to the Admissions Office for a reader's card. As a Belgian, he did not fully understand the English text of the oath he was being asked to read out, and so he asked for a version in Latin – as an inhabitant of the Vatican City this was the most appropriate vernacular language for him. A new Latin version was duly produced. This set off a programme of translating the declaration into as many languages as possible. It is currently available in over 150 languages, including Cornish and Manx.

FIRE PREVENTION

Fire prevention has always been a matter of great importance to the custodians of the Bodleian Library. This is illustrated by the following extract from the 1926 *Staff Manual*:

EXTRACT FROM THE BODLEIAN STATUTE

No person shall under any pretext bring into the Library, any fire, or any lamp or other light, or kindle any fire or strike any light therein, under pain of deprivation of any office or appointment which he may hold in the Library...

Any infringement of this prohibition should be instantly reported to the Librarian or Sub-Librarian in charge.

* *Workmen* must not bring matches into any of the library buildings.
* *Brasiers* are not allowed in Bodleian precincts. If they are used near Bodley, the Librarian should be informed and all windows and ventilators closed into which sparks could possibly be blown.
* *When heated metal is used* for repairs &c. (on the roof of Bodley, the Camera, or inside library-premises) the Bodleian cleaner or some other experienced person should be with the workmen the entire time.
* *Hot Water Pipes and radiators* must not have anything touching them.
* *The Bodleian Janitor* has to keep all windows in Bodley closed on the night of Nov. 5 and at all other times when watchmen are engaged. And on ordinary days he has to see that all exterior windows of the library are closed.
* *Bonfires and fireworks.* The Librarian will at all times be greatly obliged for information as to the likelihood of any special celebrations taking place near the

Bodleian. They are most likely to take place in
'Torpids week' and 'Eights week'.*
* *Inflammable material* such as turpentine or oil may not
be kept in any premises occupied by Bodleian books.
* *Coal* (including all other forms of carbon e.g. coke,
anthracite, lignite and briquettes) should be stored as
far as practicable from any flues, stoves, coils, warm
pipes, warm walls, or cinderheaps, and the stock must
be kept as low as is reasonably practicable.

READER NUMBERS

With the continuing expansion of both the University and the
Library, reader numbers have grown enormously. The chang-
ing reader numbers per year over time are shown below:

YEAR	READERS
1602	248
1945	700
1952	2,500
1992	12,600
2014	64,242

In 1952/3 three-quarters of new readers were members
of the University but by 1992/3 this had gone down to a
third. By 1957 the Bodleian could house a greater number
of readers than any other university library in Britain, with
spaces for 1,117 readers. All members of staff and students
at the university are entitled to a reader's card. Anyone else
wishing to gain access to the Library must first visit the

---

* Torpids and Eights weeks are annual Oxford events whereby teams from Oxford
University compete in rowing races on the Isis (the part of the Thames that flows
through Oxford). Torpids usually takes place in the seventh week of Hilary term and
Eights is normally in the fifth week of Trinity term. Because the river is so narrow
through Oxford normal side-by-side races are not possible. Instead the races have
developed into a style called 'bumping', whereby the boats set off at a regulated
distance from one another and then race to catch and 'bump' the boat ahead. The
winning boat becomes 'Head of the River' by bumping their way to the front without
being bumped from behind.

Admissions Office to sign up for a reader's card. Scholars from other universities and those with a proven need to consult the collection may also apply for a reader's card. In 2014/15, of the 64,242 registered users, 32,053 were not members of the University. In 2014/15 there were 2,307,848 reader visits over the course of the year.

SHELFMARKS EXPLAINED

Shelfmarks are the codes given to each book, item or manuscript, which allow librarians to catalogue, shelve and then find the books. Due to the variety of systems used over the centuries to classify the books in the Bodleian (see p. 64) the shelfmarks used are not standardized. In simple terms many of the shelfmarks in the Bodleian fall into five types, thus:

1. *Names of former owners or libraries*, revealing the source of books and keeping these collections together; for example, Holkham, Selden, Douce.
2. *Categories grouped by subject matter*, for example Art, Bib(le collection), Med(icine).
3. *Groups that have a common category*, for example Don(ations), Inc(unabula), Diss(ertations). These sorts of shelfmarks group together items acquired in a particular way (like a donation) or items of a particular type (like a book printed before 1501).
4. *Groups that are described by location* within the library in which they are, or were, kept; for example Mexican case, Arch(ives cupboard), Auct(arium) (which took over the Anatomy School).
5. *Descriptions of non-books or non-typographic publications*, for example Microfiche, Copperplate, Film.

THE NINE MUSES
OF THE CLARENDON BUILDING

In Greek mythology the nine muses were ethereal beings who protected the arts and inspired mortal writers, poets, musicians and artists to create great works. In 1712–13 the Clarendon Building was built as the headquarters of Oxford University Press. It was designed by Nicholas Hawksmoor. In 1717 around the roof were placed nine lead figures of the muses by Sir James Thornhill. The muses and the art they represent are as follows:

MUSE	REPRESENTS
Calliope	*epic poetry*
Clio	*history*
Euterpe	*music & song*
Erato	*lyric poetry*
Melpomene	*tragedy*
Polyhymnia	*hymns*
Terpsichore	*dance*
Thalia	*comedy*
Urania	*astronomy*

Thomas Hearne in *Reliquiae* reports that the statues 'were at first refused, and suffered to lie at the Wharf for above two years; they cost £600'. Unfortunately when the statues were at last put in place on the roof they were not secured, relying upon their own weight to hold them in place. Consequently one of them blew down in the late eighteenth century, and another in 1810. The impact was such that the fallen statues of Euterpe and Melpomene were flattened and scrapped. The missing muses were not replaced until 1974, when fibreglass replicas made from the original drawings were created by Richard Kindersley.

BODLEIAN LIBRARIES
BY SIZE OF COLLECTION

Bodleian Libraries is the umbrella group that oversees all the dependent libraries of the Bodleian, covering subjects as diverse as plant taxonomy and Japanese. The following is a list of the dependent libraries* organized by size of collection, starting with the largest:

Weston Library
Bodleian Library
Radcliffe Science Library
Taylor Institution Library
Bodleian Law Library
Sackler Library
Bodleian Social Science Library
Taylor Bodleian
Slavonic and Modern Greek Library
Bodleian Japanese Library
Vere Harmsworth Library
at the Rothermere American Institute
English Faculty Library
Bodleian Oriental Institute Library
History Faculty Library
(in the Radcliffe Camera)
Rewley House Continuing Education Library
Leopold Muller Memorial Library
Philosophy and Theology Faculties Library
Bodleian Music Faculty Library
Bodleian Education Library
Alexander Library of Ornithology
Bodleian Health Care Libraries: Cairns
Bodleian KB Chen China Centre Library
Sainsbury Library at the Saïd Business School

---

* There are 30 dependent libraries; only 29 are included in this list since Egrove Park Library has the same stock as the Saïd Business School Library.

Bodleian Latin American Centre Library
Sherardian Library of Plant Taxonomy
Wellcome Unit for the History of Medicine Library
Bodleian Health Care Libraries: Knowledge Centre
Bodleian Health Care Libraries: Horton
Bodleian Health Care Libraries:
Nuffield Orthopaedic Centre

LEGAL DEPOSIT LIBRARIES

In 1610 Thomas Bodley reached an agreement with the
Stationers' Company of London that a copy of every book
published in England would be deposited at the Bodleian
Library, ensuring that the collection of books would be ever-
growing. This agreement was the forerunner of legal deposit,
which came into force in 1662, whereby printers were obliged
to supply the libraries of Oxford and Cambridge, in addition
to the Royal Library (now the British Library), with three
copies of every book published in the UK. This was further
reiterated under the first Copyright Act of 1709 and again in
1911. In 2003 and 2013 legal deposit was extended to include
online and digital items such as websites, blogs, CD-ROMs and
social media. The following libraries (with date they joined
in parentheses) are the six legal deposit libraries in the UK:

Bodleian Library, Oxford	1662
University Library Cambridge	1662
The British Library*	1709
National Library of Scotland†	1709
Trinity College Library, Dublin	1801
National Library of Wales	1911

---

* previously The Royal Library.
† previously Advocates Library.

The British Library is the only library which automatically receives a copy of every book published in the UK or Ireland; the other libraries are entitled to request any book published within the previous twelve months.

IMPRESSIONS OF THE EIGHTEENTH-CENTURY BODLEIAN

John Pinkerton's *A General Collection of the Best and Most Interesting Voyages and Travels in All Parts of the World* (1808) contains an account of a visit to Oxford by one Manuel Gonzales, a Portuguese merchant who apparently visited England in the 1730s and recorded his impressions of the various places he visited. Of the Bodleian he wrote:

> The Divinity school is an ancient building, not only roofed, but intirely built with free-stone. It was no less than fifty-three years in building and finishing, being begun anno 1427, and not finished till the year 1480. The work of the roof is very curious and ornamental.
>
> The Schools of Arts being built contiguous to the two ends of that part or extent of the Bodleian library, which looks eastward, make a spacious and splendid quadrangle, or square court ... On the east are the schools of geometry and arithmetick, astronomy, metaphysicks, logick; between which stands a lofty tower, the lower part of it being the great gate or porch of entrance, over which is a mathematical library for the Savilian professor; and over that, part of the school's gallery; over that, the university archives or repository for its records and writings; and at top is an astronomical observatory.

BODLEIAN TREASURES:
CODEX MENDOZA

The Codex Mendoza (MS. Arch. Selden A. 1) offers a fascinating insight into the customs of conquest-era Mexicans. Commissioned by Don Antonio de Mendoza (1491–1552), the first viceroy of New Spain (Spanish possessions in South and Central America, including Mexico, Costa Rica, Honduras, Spanish Florida and the Philippines) for Holy Roman Emperor Charles V, the book includes pictograms, annotated in Spanish, revealing Aztec daily life plus a history and tribute list of the Aztec emperors. The Codex was sent by ship from Mexico City to Spain but on its way the ship was attacked by French privateers and the Codex fell into the hands of André Thevet, geographer to Henri II of France. Thevet wrote his name a number of times into the Codex, with the date 1553. Around thirty years later English writer and geographer Richard Hakluyt bought the Codex. He later bequeathed it to his fellow travel writer Samuel Purchas. The book ended up in the collection of John Selden and was gifted, alongside the rest of his huge collection, to the Bodleian c. 1659. The Codex did not gain much scholarly attention until 1831, when it was 'rediscovered' by Viscount Kingsborough and its importance as a source on Aztec history and language was realized.

OPIE COLLECTION

Iona and Peter Opie were celebrated folklorists who dedicated their lives to collecting and preserving children's stories, rhymes and games. From 1944 the couple gathered children's literature, colouring books, comics and workbooks from the sixteenth to the twentieth century, until the collection reached over 20,000 items. This massive resource for folklorists and researchers alike was acquired by the Bodleian in 1988, half of it donated by Iona Opie, the other half bought after a public appeal for funds.

THOMAS BODLEY'S STIPULATIONS

When Sir Thomas Bodley founded the Library in 1602, he wrote out a long list of library statutes, or rules, which were to be observed. These have been changed many times during the intervening centuries, but a surprising number of Bodley's original ideas and rules have remained. Borrowing books is still strictly forbidden and the three original posts he created to run the library – Librarian or Keeper, Sub-Librarian and Janitor – still exist to this day. Some of Bodley's original stipulations (a couple of which, for obvious reasons, have since been dropped) are listed below:

* The Librarian must be celibate*
* The Library may only be closed on Sundays, Christmas Day, the day of the election of the proctors and Visitation Day
* The Library must be open from 8 a.m. to 11 a.m., and again from 2 p.m. to 5 p.m. and in the winter from 1 p.m. to 4 p.m.
* The Librarian must be there every single day and will be fined 20 shillings for any absences
* The Librarian must be a diligent student, trusty, active and discreet in his conversation, a graduate, a linguist, and not encumbered with marriage [which was considered to be too full of 'domestic impeachments']; nor could he hold a benefice of the church

---

* This stipulation was ignored by the very first Librarian, Thomas James, who married in 1602. Many other Librarians also married and so this rather futile rule was finally taken off the list of stipulations in 1847.

THE BODLEIAN IN FICTION

The Bodleian has been inspiring writers since its doors were first opened in 1602. Novels which feature the Bodleian as a setting (or encompass a fictional version of the library) include:

His Dark Materials trilogy by Philip Pullman
The Warden's Niece by Gillian Avery
Equinox by Michael White
A Discovery of Witches by Deborah Harkness
Crampton Hodnet by Barbara Pym
Operation Pax by Michael Innes
The Sword of Moses by Dominic Selwood
Gaudy Night by Dorothy L. Sayers
The Cruellest Month by Hazel Holt
The Wench is Dead by Colin Dexter

BODLEY'S WILL

Thomas Bodley's obsessive passion for the creation of a library culminated in his will. He bequeathed almost all of his money and assets to the Library and only a couple of hundred pounds each to his relations. This left nobody in any doubt as to whose survival and continued good fortune he cared about. Bodley's relatives contested the will but were not successful in altering its terms – this isn't surprising given that Bodley had appointed three of the most powerful men in the land as his executors: the Archbishop of Canterbury, the Lord Chancellor and the Lord Chief Justice. He took no chances when it came to making sure that his beloved library would be provided for after his death.

The Bodleian has always relied on the generosity of patrons to help grow the collection and preserve important texts. The Register of Benefactors (first volume) is a massive book of 448 pages listing, in double columns, the names and donations to the Library from its beginnings to 1688. The second volume records up to 1794. Each year donors were listed according to their status, rather than when they made their gift. The following is a list of some of the donations made to the library in 1603/4:

Sir Walter Raleigh	£50
Earl of Northumberland	£100
Sir Robert Cotton	11 manuscripts
John Mericke (English Consul in Russia)	2 Russian manuscripts
Sir Michael Dormer	collection of Italian books
Sir Valentine Knightley	£10
William Allen	printed books
Sir William Roper	works of Sir Thomas More
Lord Abergavenny	printed books
Earl of Nottingham	manuscripts and printed books
Sir George More	30 manuscripts and £40 (used to buy 89 books and 2 manuscripts)
Sir George Sayntpoll	£20
William Ballow	15 manuscripts

BODLEIAN TREASURES:
THE GUTENBERG BIBLE

The Gutenberg Bible (c. 1455) was the first major book to be printed with movable type, signalling the start of the age of the printed book. Before this, all books were copied by hand by scribes, or meticulously printed with wooden blocks, meaning that it could take months to produce just one copy of a book. Between 160 and 180 copies of the Gutenberg Bible were printed, but today only 49 survive and of these only 21 are complete (although debate exists on the exact numbers). It is considered to be one of the most valuable books in the world – the last time one sold in 1978 it went for $2.2 million. The Bodleian's copy (Arch. B b.10, 11, two volumes) was bought for £100 in 1793, which at that time was a huge amount, making up one-fifth of the Library's book-buying budget.

JOURNALS, NEWSPAPERS AND MAGAZINES

As a legal deposit library the Bodleian is entitled to receive copies of a number of newspapers, magazines and journals. Within the Library these are known as serial titles, as they are items which come regularly into the collection. Below are a number of statistics about the serial titles collected in 2014/15:

Number of serial titles in print only	28,318
Number of serial titles in electronic form only	73,395
Number of serial titles in print and electronic form	7,873
Total number of serial titles available electronically to users	81,268
Number of legal deposit print serial titles	26,268
Number of electronic legal deposit serial titles	4,457
Total number of legal deposit serial titles	30,725
Total number of serial titles	109,586

A register to record visitors* to the library was kept by the first Bodley's Librarian, Thomas James, from the very first day the Bodleian opened. Thomas James's Register can still be viewed in the library today (MS. Bodl. 763). Readers' names were written down in alphabetical order followed by the dates they came to the library, with an *a* to show they came in the morning, and a *p* to show they were there in the afternoon – the library was closed between 11 a.m. and 1 p.m. each day. The register shows that three people came on the day it opened – the morning of 8 November 1602, including a Mr Day of Oriel College. It was clearly a lot of work to keep the register updated and this is probably why it ends just a year later on 7 November 1603. During this first year there was a daily average of 17 readers, with numbers increasing towards the end of the register, so that for the last few days it records 30 names. In total 248 readers are listed: 20 of those were visitors and 19 were described as *Extranei*, meaning foreign – which indicated that they came from outside the University and used the Library with special dispensation. Of these, 15 were from Europe – including 3 from France, 2 from Denmark, 2 from Silesia (now part of Poland), 2 from Prussia, 1 from Switzerland and 1 from Saxony.

---

* A glimpse into the seventeenth-century Library is provided by a small notebook which survives in the archives of the Bodleian. The notebook reveals the names of the readers in 1648–9 for whom the sub-librarian fetched books. The notebook indicates that 218 of the readers during that period were university scholars with an M.A. or higher status, 99 were B.A.s, two were students of civil law visiting from London, and three were from overseas.

BODLEIAN TREASURES:
THE FIRST TRADE AGREEMENT
BETWEEN JAPAN AND ENGLAND

Dated 12 October 1613 (NS), this document (MS. Jap. b.2) in Japanese calligraphy was an agreement between Shogun Tokugawa Ieyasu and the English East India Company for privileges to trade with Japan. The manuscript is a *shuinjo* (vermilion seal document), one of only two handed to English Captain John Saris during his eighth voyage aboard the *Clove*. The Bodleian's *shuinjo* is the only version of the trade agreement known to survive and has been in the Bodleian's collection since at least 1680.

THE FIRST SHELFMARKS

When the Bodleian Library was first opened in 1602 the books and manuscripts were classified by just four shelfmarks based on subject, which indicated where on the shelves a book could be found. Samples of the earliest Bodleian shelfmarks by subject are as follows:

A 1.4 Th. (Theology) | B 1.15 Med. (Medicine)
4° M 8 Jur. (Jurisprudence) | 8° W 18 Art.*

The first of these is an example of a Th. shelfmark. Thus for A 1.4 Th. the first letter indicates that it is a folio volume (as it has no size prefix, 4° or 8°) whose author's surname begins with A, it is kept on the first shelf (1) and is fourth book on that shelf in the A grouping in the Theology section.

---

* The volumes you would find with these shelfmarks are as follows: A 1.4 Th. is volume 4 of a 10-volume set of *St. Augustine's Opera* (Basel, 1528–9); B 1.15 Med. refers to *Mattioli's Opera* (Frankfurt, 1598); 4° M 8 Jur. is *Practica iudiciaria* (Magdeburg, 1606); and 8° W 18 Art. is *Contemplationum physicarum sectio* (Hanover, 1625).

THE FRIEZE

An enormous painted frieze decorates the internal walls of the upper floor in the Schools Quadrangle. It features portraits of 202 writers, depicting a history of learning. The frieze was painted in 1619 under the guidance of the first Librarian, Thomas James, and represents an especially Protestant view of scholarship.* The portraits featured in the frieze include:

Homer | Sappho† | Geoffrey Chaucer
Sir Philip Sidney | Tycho Brahe | Thomas Aquinas
Peter Lombard | Martin Bucer | Ulrich Zwingli
John Calvin | Desiderius Erasmus | Martin Luther
Andreas Vesalius | Hippocrates | Virgil | Euclid
Livy | Pliny | Strabo | Nicolas Copernicus | Ovid
Dante | Aristotle | Plato | Thomas Cranmer
Bernard of Clairvaux

Unfortunately the roof above the frieze was so badly designed that water leaked in and dissolved the water-based pigments in the paint. Despite numerous attempts to fix the roof and restore the portraits the frieze was in such a bad state that in 1830 it was decided that the walls should be panelled and plastered over, damaging it yet further. The frieze was uncovered in 1949 and was restored to its former glory; it is still inspiring readers in the Upper Reading Room today.

---

* Thomas James was strongly Protestant and, following Bodley's lead, envisaged the library as a centre of Protestant learning – so much so that he was rumoured to have recommended consulting the papal *Index of Prohibited Books* as a useful reference of books to stock.

† The Ancient Greek poet Sappho is the only woman included in the frieze.

A YEAR IN THE BODLEIAN IN NUMBERS

One of the best ways to gain an insight into the work of the Bodleian Library is to consider a year* in the life of the Bodleian Libraries in numbers:

Total additions to printed stock in a year	251,924
Purchased/subscribed books and serials added	121,065
Items added via legal deposit	128,298
Maps added	2,561
Number of items of printed stock disposed of	73,457
Total catalogued printed stock	11,910,646
Metres of archives and manuscripts received in a year	269
Total number of loans†	2,005,283
Number of items from special collections consulted	68,848
Views of digitized book or manuscript from the website	220,587
Reader visits	2,368,327
Average number of readers in the libraries at 11.30 a.m.	1,307
Total number of enquiries during a week	9,327
Number of items catalogued	112,340
Library catalogue (SOLO) searches	11,975,375
Shop sales	£732,000
Books moved	35 km
Books repaired	1,000
Conservation boxes made	26,000
Items treated in conservation workshop	9,113
Items ingested into the Book Storage Facility‡	311,994
Fetches from the Book Storage Facility	237,921

---

* The statistics used here are for the year 2014/15.

† These statistics cover all the libraries in the Bodleian Library group (see p. 14 for a list of all the dependent libraries) and so, although readers cannot borrow books from the main Bodleian Library, this figure represents the books borrowed from the libraries within the group that allow loans.

‡ See p. 30.

GEORGIAN COLLECTION

The Bodleian has the greatest collection of Georgian manuscripts outside Russia, and this is mainly thanks to the
efforts of scholars Sir Oliver Wardrop and his sister Marjory
Wardrop. The Wardrops worked hard to translate and in-
troduce Georgian culture to Britain after living there when
Oliver was Chief Commissioner of the Transcaucasus (a
region incorporating, among others, Armenia, Georgia and
Azerbaijan). When Marjory died in 1909, her brother set up
a fund for the encouragement of Georgian studies, through
which all of her papers and books were given to the Bodleian. He also gave further donations of his own books and
manuscripts throughout the rest of his life. Among these are
two wonderful seventeenth-century manuscripts of the late-
twelfth-century Georgian epic poem *The Knight in the Panther Skin*
by Shota Rustaveli. In June 2014 both of these manuscripts
were added to the UNESCO Memory of the World Register.

BODLEIAN TREASURES:
SHAKESPEARE'S FIRST FOLIO

Thomas Bodley's contemptuous opinion of English literature
meant that the Library did not hold any works by William
Shakespeare until 1623. In that year, what is known as the
First Folio was published and a copy came to the Library,
unbound, possibly as part of the agreement made with the
Stationers' Company that a copy of every book published in
England would be given to the library (see p. 15). This was
the first collected edition of Shakespeare's plays, collated and
edited by his old friends and fellow actors John Heminge
and Henry Condell. They divided the thirty-six plays into
Comedies, Tragedies and Histories, the way of grouping
them that persists to this day. The First Folio remained in
the Library until 1664 when the Third Folio was published
with its seven extra plays – at this point it is possible that the

First Folio was seen as superfluous and probably sold off as a 'duplicate' copy in order to raise funds. In those days the idea of the importance of first editions had not yet taken root, and nobody had any idea that it would be recognized as one of the most important books in the English language.

However, by strange coincidence, in 1905 an undergraduate named Turbutt brought to the library a First Folio which had been in his family for five generations and was now very battered and worn, keen to get advice on repairing the old volume, which was fortunately still in its original binding. Within minutes library staff had established beyond all doubt that this was the very copy that had once belonged to the library. All they had to do now was get it back again. This process was not made easier or less expensive by the fact that the great American Shakespearean collector Henry Folger had somehow got wind of the find and was determined to get hold of it himself. There was a mad scramble to raise funds at the Bodleian so that they could match Folger's dizzying bid of £3,000. This included an open letter in *The Times* by the thirteenth Bodley's Librarian Nicholson begging for donations. At the eleventh hour the money was raised and the Folio was returned to its old home in Oxford.

BOOKS IN OTHER LANGUAGES

The Bodleian collection has books in many languages from around the world. The top five most common languages represented by number of books in the collection are as follows:

1. English
2. German
3. French
4. Chinese
5. Italian

CLEANING ROTA FOR 1904

Keeping the library clean has been a constant preoccupation ever since the Bodleian first opened. By 1904 a detailed rota of what was to be cleaned and when was listed along with various other duties for Library staff in what was known as the *Staff-Kalendar*. The rota in 1904 was as follows:

MONDAY 4 JANUARY 1904

Preparation of staff reports of work for 1903 to begin
Bodley clocks to be wound
[Radcliffe] Camera clock to be wound
Boys' time sheets for last week to be made up
Janitors' fee book to be initialled by Librarian
Reports on boys to be sent in
Overtime statements to be sent in and entered
Sutherland room to be cleaned
Old Ashmolean stairs and back and front areas to be
    cleaned
Camera accession lists to be copied at Bodley

Every member of staff was given their own copy of the *Kalendar* and encouraged to put a mark in red ink beside those duties that specifically concerned them.

BODLEIAN TREASURES: *DON QUIXOTE*

When Thomas Bodley first set up his library he sent trusted booksellers to Europe to buy important contemporary works. One such bookseller was John Bill, who was sent to Spain in 1605 and came back with, among others, a first edition of Miguel de Cervantes's *Don Quixote* (Arch. B e.53). Bound in its original vellum cover, the now extremely rare book was rather smaller than the folios housed in Duke Humfrey's Library and so was soon placed in the gallery of Arts End, where new shelving for smaller books had been built.

THE BODLEIAN IN FILM AND TELEVISION

The extraordinary architecture of the Bodleian has made it a popular location for film-makers in recent years. Three of the Harry Potter blockbusters were filmed there, with the Divinity School becoming the Hogwarts Infirmary and Duke Humfrey's as the library. When filming *Harry Potter and the Philosopher's Stone* the cast had to cram in a marathon 43-hour filming session in Duke Humfrey's Library so as to not disrupt readers. The shoot began at 1 p.m. on Saturday 21 October 2000, when the last readers left, and pushed on through until 8 a.m. on the Monday morning – just one hour before the room was opened to readers again. Other movies filmed at the Bodleian include:

X-Men: Days of Future Past (2014)
The Golden Compass (2007)
Another Country (1984)
The History Boys (2006)
The Madness of King George III (1994)
Pocahontas: The New World (2005)
Shadowlands (1993)
To Kill a King (2003)

The library has also featured in several television shows, including:

Inspector Morse
Lewis
Brideshead Revisited
William & Mary
Melvyn Bragg's *12 Books that Changed the World*
Stephen Fry's *Fry's Planet Word*
David Starkey's *Monarchy*

THE BOOK STORAGE FACILITY

By 2005 the bookstack of the New Bodleian with 3.5 million books was full and the storage facility at Nuneham Courtenay was also at capacity with 1.3 million books. To solve this, in 2010 the purpose-built £26 million Book Storage Facility (BSF) in South Marston, just outside Swindon, was opened. The BSF was built to allow the storage of huge numbers of low-usage items, taking the pressure off the sites in central Oxford and allowing the refurbishment of the Weston Library as a special collections and research library. The site holds books, periodicals, maps, manuscripts, newspapers and microfilm, mostly from the eighteenth century onwards. In numbers:

Miles of shelving	146
Capacity	12–13 million items
Number of crates/totes to circulate material	1,000
Number of forklift trucks operating in warehouse	7
Number of new items arriving each day	1,000
By December 2015 it held	9,503,788 items
Reader requests retrieved by December 2015	1,050,000
Vans travel* from Swindon to Oxford with retrieved items	twice a day
One millionth book request processed† through BSF	6 October 2015

---

* Each year the van carries 187 tonnes of books requested by readers to and from the BSF.

† The book requested was *Aristophanes* by James Robson, and was requested at the Sackler Library by Classics scholar Aneurin Ellis-Evans, a Junior Research Fellow at The Queen's College. To celebrate this milestone, the twenty-fifth Bodley's Librarian,

BODLEIAN TREASURES:
THE BAY PSALM BOOK

The Bay Psalm Book was the first book to be printed in North America. In 1638 a Cambridge locksmith, Stephen Day, travelled to Cambridge, Massachusetts, with paper and printing press in order to set up the first printing press in the new American colony. By 1640 Day had published the first complete book, *The Whole Booke of Psalmes Faithfully Translated into English Metre* (now known as the Bay Psalm Book, after the Massachusetts Bay settlement), of which 1,700 copies were produced. Today only 11 survive, and the Bodleian's copy (Arch. G e.40) is the only one outside North America. One of the two copies owned by Old South Church, Boston, Massachusetts, was sold at auction in New York in 2013 for $14.2 million, becoming the most expensive printed book ever sold. A facsimile of the Bodleian's copy was published in 2014.

CATALOGUING CARROLL

Charles Lutwidge Dodgson, lecturer in mathematics at Christ Church, was keen to keep his pen name a secret. As Lewis Carroll, Dodgson had published the hugely popular *Alice's Adventures in Wonderland* (1865), but he was also a brilliant mathematician, writing academic treatises on geometry, and he was determined to keep the two personas entirely separate. Unfortunately, the zealous compilers of the Bodleian catalogue cross-referenced the two names (as was standard), so that anyone looking up Charles Dodgson could see that he also wrote under the name Lewis Carroll and vice versa. Dodgson was furious when he discovered this and immediately demanded that the entries be changed so as to preserve his secret, but sticking to its standard cataloguing system the Library refused.

Richard Ovenden, presented Dr Ellis-Evans with a catalogue from the *Marks of Genius* exhibition held at the Weston Library.

BODLEIAN SUPERLATIVES

SMALLEST BOOK   At the time of publication *Old King Cole*, published by Gleniffer Press in 1985, is the tiniest book in the library at just 90 mm high. This book was verified as the smallest book in the world printed using offset lithography* by the *Guinness Book of Records*. The nursery rhyme Old King Cole is spread across twelve single pages and printed on the finest 22 gsm English paper.

LARGEST BOOK   *Birds of America* by John James Audubon is one of the largest books in the collection. This beautifully illustrated work published in 1827–38 contains 435 hand-painted engravings which Audubon insisted be life-sized (and therefore needed to be big enough for a to-scale illustration of an eagle). Printed on the largest available paper size (known as double elephant folio), it measures roughly 39.5 by 28.5 inches.

LONGEST BOOK   One of the longest items in the collection is *Sumiyoshi monogatari: Tale of Sumiyoshi* (MS.Jap.c.8(r)) in three scrolls (1,680 cm, 1,426 cm, 1,631 cm = total 4,731 cm). The scroll is an anonymous tale of the early Kamakura period (1185–1333) which resembles the Cinderella story. The scroll was probably produced in the mid-Edo period (1688–1788). It was donated by Paget J. Toynbee (1855–1932) in 1912.

A printed roll of the Bayeux Tapestry is one of the longest books in the collection at over 7 metres. It was published by the Society of Antiquaries of London in 1823 – originally as flat leaves in a large book, but a former owner (possibly Francis Douce) cut it up into strips, stuck it to a linen backing and turned it into a roll.

---

* Offset printing is when a book is printed by transferring the inked image from a metal plate to a rubber roller and from there onto paper.

RAREST BOOK   There are many unique books in the collection. One of the most recently acquired is *The Troops*, a wonderful account of a group of seventeen childhood friends and their escapades from 1923 to 1929, growing up together in the idyllic Sussex Downs. The book, lovingly hand-produced in 1935, includes charming hand-pasted photographs of the group, offering a fascinating insight into a 1920s childhood. It is the only copy known to have survived.

MOST EXPENSIVE PRINTED BOOK   The Bay Psalm Book (see p. 31), the first book to be printed in North America in 1640, is the most expensive printed book in the collection verified at sale. Only 11 copies of the book survive. One was recently sold at auction in New York for $14.2 million (£8.8 million).

MOST EXPENSIVE SINGLE ACQUISITION   The Bodleian's most expensive single acquisition was a copy of the autograph draft manuscript of Jane Austen's unfinished novel *The Watsons* (see p. 46). The manuscript cost over £1 million; the acquisition was made possible by a grant from the National Heritage Memorial Fund (NHMF) and the generous help of many of the Library's supporters. Historically other (at the time) expensive acquisitions include Shakespeare's First Folio (see p. 26), purchased for £3,000 (roughly £326,000 in today's money) in 1905, and the first Gutenberg Bible (see p. 21), purchased in 1793 for £100 (about £250,000 today).

LARGEST AND SMALLEST LIBRARIES   The largest library by reader spaces is the Old Bodleian Library and Gladstone Link, with 702 reader spaces. The smallest is the modest Wellcome Unit for the History of Medicine Library, with 5 reader spaces.

MOST POPULAR ITEM IN THE BODLEIAN SHOP   Leather bookmark: 9,366 sold in 2014/15.

MOST BORROWED BOOK   In 2014/15 the most borrowed book was *EU Law: Text, Cases and Materials* by Paul P. Craig, 5th edition, 2011.[*]

WEEKLY TASKS FROM 1919

The *Staff Manual* from 1919 lists all the tasks the staff of the Bodleian Library were expected to attend to on a weekly basis. A selection of weekly tasks are laid out below:

MONDAY

Bodley clocks to be wound and set
Librarian's room to be dusted
Personal report of cataloguing, revising, classifying,
    handlisting and labelling at [Radcliffe] Camera
Ashes to be removed from Bodley furnaces

TUESDAY

Ashes to be removed from Camera
Report of cataloguing, revising, classifying, handlisting
    and labelling at Bodley
Bodley reserve study to be weeded out
Proscholium to be swept

WEDNESDAY

Report on crossing off of dead order-slips
Bodley and Camera suggestion-books to be examined
Mr Wiblin to send books for binding
Orders for coke to be sent

THURSDAY

Report on state of transcribing, revising of transcription,
    mounting, cutting up, arranging, 'ticking in', pasting,
    and entering (*gen. catal. of pr. bks.*)

---

[*] Borrowing is not allowed from the main Bodleian Library but is allowed at many of the dependent libraries. All of the top five most borrowed books in 2014/15 were law books.

Bills to be filed
Envelopes &c. to be written for posting
Lavatory in Quad to be swept out

FRIDAY
Cheques to be paid
Cash-book and ledger to be posted up
Bodley front staircases to be cleaned

SATURDAY
Foreign book orders to be sent
New foreign books to be catalogued
Top blinds of S. window of Arts-end to be drawn down
    at night

CATALOGUES

The first printed catalogue for the Library was produced in
1605 – it was made up of manuscripts as well as books. The
1605 catalogue reveals that at that time there were very few
items in the collection in the English language, demonstrat-
ing that most scholarly works were still written in classical
languages and reflecting Bodley's view that items in English
were not good enough to be stored in an academic library.

By 1620 a new edition of the catalogue was required.
The collection had grown to such an extent that the 1620
catalogue came to 675 pages; it was the first book catalogue
to list all the books alphabetically by author.

Thomas Hyde was the fifth Bodley's Librarian. He worked
hard to create a catalogue of all the books in the library,
which was completed in 1674. It was a labour of love. Hyde
wrote in the preface to the catalogue how hard it had been
working in the unheated library and how little appreciated
his cataloguing skills were. Such was the quality of Hyde's
catalogue that it was used as a basis for many other library
catalogues – indeed the Mazarin Library in Paris annotated
and used their copy of the 1674 Bodleian catalogue up until
1760.

In 1843 the new printed catalogue of the collection reached three folio volumes – it was the last version of the catalogue that was physically printed.

The twelfth Librarian Henry Coxe introduced a new cataloguing system in 1859, a system which would prove more flexible as the collection continued to grow. The 'movable slip' method was borrowed from the British Museum. It involved writing each catalogue entry on a slip of paper, which was then pasted into blank pages; the slip could then be moved as new entries were added to the catalogue. Three slips were needed for each book – one for the main catalogue in Arts End, one for the Radcliffe Camera catalogue and one for the subject catalogue.

In the mid-nineteenth century a vicar named Alfred Hackman (1811–1874), who became sub-librarian, was assigned to work on the 1843 catalogue, its supplement and the new transcribed catalogue. The story goes that Hackman was but a small man, and so to sit at his desk comfortably he sat atop a copy of the *Chronicon Gotwicense*. Once the New Catalogue 1859–1874 had been completed – a work of many hands – it was discovered that it was missing one vital volume from the collection: the very one Hackman had been sitting on for thirty-six years, the *Chronicon Gotwicense*.

The published catalogue is the formal face of the Library and so may not include everything actually in the collection. The handlists (i.e. shelf lists) and guardbooks were a much more accurate representation of the collection. Up until 1992 the huge guardbooks were still used to record all the items in the library by cataloguers cutting and pasting entries into place. Due to the size of the collection the guardbooks took up a whole room in the library. Today they are preserved (but not added to) in Swindon.

In 1988 the catalogue was switched to an electronic cataloguing system. The current book catalogue is called SOLO. The software used to create the electronic catalogue has developed and improved over the years and has become more standardized. The current system is called ALEPH and uses machine-readable cataloguing (MARC), a system which most libraries around the world use today, meaning that data can be more easily shared among institutions.

Today cataloguing is a much more cooperative venture, and the Bodleian catalogue includes information from all the dependent libraries, most of the college libraries, plus the Oxford Union and Oxford Centre for Islamic Studies. The collaborative nature of the catalogue means that currently over 200 people are working on keeping the catalogue up to date.

The Bodleian cataloguers contribute to the international approved list of subject headings overseen by the Library of Congress, which are used to describe the books catalogued in libraries across the world. The latest subject headings suggested by the Bodleian cataloguers included: 'Air source heat pump systems' and 'Jaguar automobile in art'.

CONSERVING BOOKS

A team of conservators work in a specially built studio in the new Weston Library to repair and protect the books and manuscripts in the collection. Below are some facts about this fascinating team:

Number of conservators	16, plus 3 assistants and 3 technicians
Length of training	2-year full-time M.A. in conservation*
Number of items conserved each year	8,000–12,000
Most common issues resolved	detached spines, edge tears, loose pages, stuck pages, consolidation of loose painted media
Most useful pieces of conservation kit	the humidity cabinet, the fume cupboard and the AG2000 misting system to consolidate fragile media.

---

* To work in a top conservation unit such as the one at the Bodleian, a conservator would have to have six–eight years of experience from internships and project work on top of the two-year M.A. before they reached the level required..

The Divinity School was built between 1427 and 1483 and is the oldest surviving room purpose-built for the use of the University of Oxford. Theology was taught and examined there under the Gothic vaulted ceiling, with 455 carved stone bosses (see p. 42). Duke Humfrey's Library is housed directly above the Divinity School and by 1700 the weight of the books began to tell on the structure. The Library was examined and the book presses were found to have moved a rather alarming 9 cm, the south wall was 19 cm out of kilter, and the four arches of the Divinity School were badly cracked. The advice of Sir Christopher Wren was urgently sought. He recommended a programme of adding buttresses at ground-floor level, filling cracks with wood and plaster of Paris, and improving the drainage and guttering to prevent damp soaking into the foundations. These works were carried out in 1701–02. This was not the first time Sir Christopher Wren had made his mark on the Divinity School: in 1669, when building the Sheldonian Theatre, Wren decided the Divinity School needed a number of tweaks to better serve his grand design. Wren had a door built into the north wall to allow processions of academics to pass easily from the Divinity School (where robes are donned) to the Sheldonian (where university ceremonies take place). Just to make it clear who had made this change to the building, Wren had the letters C.W.A placed above the door (standing for Christopher Wren, architect).

The Divinity School (and Proscholium) did not come into the Bodleian's hands until 1968, when they were made available as exhibition spaces, enticing 64,000 visitors in 1968, rising to 400,000 by 1985. Today the Divinity School is part of the guided tour of the Library and contains three fascinating pieces of furniture. The first is Sir Thomas Bodley's chest, which until 1774 was used to store money and is painted with the coat of arms of both Bodley and the University. The second item is a 'mathematical chest' given to the Library by

Sir Henry Savile. The chest, which has four locks, was used to store the money which supported the professorships of Geometry and Astronomy. The final item is a chair made from timber from Sir Francis Drake's ship *The Golden Hind*, in which he circumnavigated the globe.

SIZE OF THE COLLECTION

As the collection is endlessly growing, recording its size is something of a Sisyphean task – made more so by the fact that the collection can be measured by number of books, number of volumes, or indeed number of printed items. Thus the totals in the list below are not directly comparable, as the unit of measurement changes; but it gives a glimpse into the astonishing growth of the collection, in its many guises.

1488	281 manuscripts
1602	2,500 volumes
1845*	250,000 volumes
1914	1,000,000 volumes
1951	2,000,000 volumes
1986	5,000,000 volumes
2002	7,000,000 volumes
2015	12,000,000 printed items (includes modern books, rare books, maps and music)

* In the early eighteenth century the Library had very little money to spend on buying new books and for the first three years there are no records of any books purchased at all. Thereafter roughly £9 a year was spent buying books, falling to an average of £7 a year by the 1730s.

THE TRANSIT OF VENUS

In 1769 Thomas Hornsby, Savilian Professor of Astronomy at the University of Oxford, observed the transit of Venus (when Venus travels between the Earth and the Sun so that it is visible on the latter as a small black disc) over the Tower of the Five Orders at the Bodleian Library. He wrote in *Philosophical Transactions* of his observation, comparing it to an earlier observation of the same phenomenon he had made at Shirburn Castle, Oxfordshire. This observation was vital in helping to produce the first realistic estimates of the size of the solar system. In 1772 Hornsby helped set up the Radcliffe Observatory and in 1783 became Radcliffe Librarian. Such was Hornsby's contribution to astronomy that the Hornsby crater on the moon was named in his honour.

THE RAWLINSON COLLECTION

In 1755 the library succeeded in securing the manuscripts of the collector Richard Rawlinson. The ninth Bodley's Librarian Humphrey Owen had taken great pains to woo Rawlinson to ensure his extensive collection of over 5,000 manuscripts would be bequeathed to the Library. Initially half of his collection was to be left to the Society of Antiquaries, but they foolishly let Rawlinson's politics put them off, and removed him from the Society's council because of his Jacobite sympathies. As a result Rawlinson altered his will and left most of his vast collection to the Bodleian. Rawlinson was so scrupulous in his quest to preserve historical papers that he not only bought books and manuscripts from the usual channels but also bought scrap paper by the weight from grocers and chandlers and from these secured a number of historical records, which he had bound into volumes. One of the many copperplates collected by Rawlinson, the Williamsburg Plate, was an engraving depicting Williamsburg from the period when it was the capital of the Virginia Colony (1699–1780).

The plate was used for reference in the early twentieth century when the public buildings of Williamsburg were being restored, in part due to a grant from John D. Rockefeller. In 1937 Oxford University presented John D. Rockefeller with the Williamsburg Plate in gratitude for his support of the New Bodleian Library.

INSCRIPTIONS AND STATUES OF NOTE

There are many inscriptions and statues across the Library buildings, including the following:

An inscription above the door in the entrance to the Old Library reads:

QUOD FELICITER VORTAT ACADEMICI OXONIENS(ES)
BIBLIOTHECAM HANC VOBIS REIPUBLICAEQUE
LITERATORUM T. B. P.

which translates as 'That it might turn out happily, Oxonian academics, for you and for the republic of lettered men Thomas Bodley placed this library.'

In front of the Library entrance stands a bronze statue of the third Earl of Pembroke, William Herbert, who was Chancellor of Oxford University 1617–30 and bought for the Library its first important collection of Greek manuscripts (MSS. Barocci). This statue was created by the French Huguenot sculptor Hubert le Sueur and was originally housed at the Earl of Pembroke's ancestral home, Wilton House.* It was later moved to the Bodleian, where

---

* The statue was gifted to the Library in 1723; according to one story a certain amount of persuasion was used to secure its donation. Apparently two Oxford University students dined with the seventh Earl of Pembroke at Wilton House and over the course of the meal managed to convince the earl to donate the statue to Oxford in honour of his great-uncle's links to the University. The students, perhaps worried the earl may go back on his word, reportedly returned to Oxford with the removable head of the statue to ensure the rest would follow.

it was first placed in the top-floor room under the tower, then moved to its more prominent position in the Library entrance in 1950.

In 1620 the completed Tower of the Five Orders was further enhanced by a statue of King James I, who had presented to the University a book of his collected writings. The statue representing James holds books on which the following is inscribed: HAEC HABEO QUAE SCRIPSI, HAEC HABEO QUAE DEDI, which translates as 'These things I have which I have written. These things I have which I have given.'

The vaulted ceiling of the Divinity School has 455 stone bosses, carved with inscriptions or coats of arms, including the three wheatsheaves of the Bishop of London, Thomas Kemp, who donated a large portion of the money for the building, and 'WO' representing William Orchard, the stonemason who oversaw the project. Further traditional carvings feature the Virgin and Child, the Trinity and the Evangelists, and some more unusual depictions include a fox carrying off a goose and a man picking grapes.

In 1951–52 Mark Batten, president of the Royal Society of British Sculptors, carved some new stone portrait heads of contemporary Oxford figures, such as Sir Edmund Craster, the sixteenth Bodley's Librarian 1931–45, onto the doorways on the north and south sides of the quadrangle.

In 2009 Oxford-based children's author Philip Pullman unveiled nine new grotesques on the north-west wall of the Bodleian. The new carvings were designed by local schoolchildren in a competition to replace old crumbled gargoyles. The winning designs were then sculpted by Oxfordshire stone carvers Alec and Fiona Peever. These included heads of Tweedledee and Tweedledum, Sir Thomas Bodley, Aslan, the Green Man, and General Pitt Rivers.

The atrium of the Weston Library includes an ornamental Elizabethan arch, salvaged from Ascott Park in Oxfordshire. The gate, which led to the garden of the Dorner family estate, is all that remains of the building, which was destroyed by fire in 1662. It contains a Latin inscription which reads SI BONUS ES INTRES, SI NEQUAM NE QUAQUAM – 'If you are good, enter. If wicked, by no means.'

TRADITIONAL SUBJECTS

The rooms in the Schools Quadrangle are arranged hierarchically by subject and have their names in Latin painted above the doors, revealing which subjects were studied at Oxford in the seventeenth century:

JURISPRUDENCE* | ANATOMY | METAPHYSICS
MORAL PHILOSOPHY | NATURAL PHILOSOPHY
LANGUAGES | GRAMMAR | RHETORIC†
LOGIC | ARITHMETIC | GEOMETRY
MUSIC | ASTRONOMY

Additionally students could take Theology, which was taught in the Divinity School.

GOUGH COLLECTION

Richard Gough (1735–1809) was one of the foremost antiquaries and collectors of his day. Gough was a passionate topographer and went on annual tours throughout Britain, taking copious notes and employing artists such as James Basire to illustrate his work, of which *British Topography* (1768) was his most celebrated. Throughout his life Gough had collected maps and engravings, amassing a truly impressive collection that the Bodleian was keen to acquire. The tenth

---

* The study of the theory of law.
† The art of effective and persuasive speaking or writing.

Bodley's Librarian, John Price, was intent on wooing Gough, and sent him many letters assuring him his collection would be suitably housed in the Antiquarians' Study and that he might set any conditions he liked to his gift. Gough remained non-committal and it was only on his death that the Bodleian discovered he had indeed left his extensive collection of maps and engravings to the Library, creating a starting point for one of the foremost topographical collections in the world.

BODLEIAN TREASURES: TOLKIEN'S ILLUSTRATIONS

The Bodleian holds a number of the hand-drawn illustrations crafted for The Hobbit by J.R.R. Tolkien himself. One of the most beautiful is a watercolour entitled 'Conversation with Smaug' (MS. Tolkien drawings 30) in which an invisible Bilbo converses with the huge red dragon Smaug, as he sits atop his pile of treasure. The Hobbit was first published in 1937 and contained a number of black-and-white line drawings by Tolkien. The American publishers required colour pictures for their edition, and Tolkien painted five original watercolours in the summer vacation of 1937, including 'Conversation with Smaug'.

OPENING HOURS

Before reliable timepieces it was difficult for Library staff to keep strict opening and closing hours. In the early 1600s the Library was supposed to be open from 8 to 11 a.m. and then 2 to 5 p.m. in the spring and summer or 1 to 4 p.m in the autumn and winter. To try to keep opening hours regular, in 1604 Thomas Bodley provided the first librarian, Thomas James, with a bell* which could be rung to signal both the opening and the closing of the library. However, regular opening hours continued to be a problem, and in

---

* This first bell did not come up to scratch, so it was replaced by a new bell in 1611.

1636 the University proposed that to ensure the students got their full quota of study the Librarian should turn over a three-hour sand glass in a conspicuous spot, so that students might be aware of the time they had left. One of the greatest impediments to increasing opening hours was the lack of light. Understandably, Thomas Bodley was insistent that no flame or fire should ever be used to light the Library, writing in his first draft of the library statutes:

> Be it always here provided, That for the greater security of the timber Works and Books, no frequenter of that place, Graduat or other, nor the Keeper himself, or any Deputy for him, upon any Pretext or Colour, shall enter there by Night, with a Torch, Link, Lamp, Candle, or other kind of Fire-light, upon pain of Deprivation from his Office for ever.

In 1787 the opening hours were still causing issues, with Bodley's Librarian, John Price, roundly criticized in a pamphlet *Memorial concerning the State of the Bodleian Library and the Conduct of its Principal Librarian* written by Oxford scholar Thomas Beddoes (see p. 7). Beddoes found that his hours of study in the Library were often cut short by poor timekeeping by John Price, who, although he was supposed to open the library at 8 a.m., frequently did not appear until gone 9 a.m. Bulkeley Bandinel, eleventh Bodley's Librarian from 1813 to 1860, approved new Library statutes in 1813 which extended the opening hours to 9–4 p.m. in the summer and 10–3 p.m in the winter.

It was not until 1905 that the first electric lights were installed in the Radcliffe Camera and 1929 in the Old Library, so that opening hours could be more fully extended, adding an extra two hours in the summer and four hours in the winter. Today, during the University of Oxford Terms, the Old Library is open seven days a week, 9 a.m. to 10 p.m. on weekdays, with reduced hours at the weekends. Two dependent libraries, the Cairns and the Nuffield Orthopaedic Centre (NOC) Library, are open twenty-four hours a day.

BODLEIAN TREASURES:
JANE AUSTEN'S EARLY WRITINGS

In 1933 the Bodleian acquired a small notebook full of Jane Austen's early writing (MS. Don. e. 7). 'Volume the First' contains amusing short stories Austen wrote between the ages of twelve and fifteen, which she copied out neatly when she was eighteen in 1793. The works reveal the budding writer's satirical humour beginning to develop. In 2011 the Library acquired most of Austen's draft of an unfinished novel which Jane was thought to have penned 1804–07. The 68-page draft (MS. Eng. e. 3764) is densely written with revisions and corrections throughout, providing a fascinating glimpse of the writer at work. Despite its unfinished nature it was posthumously published as The Watsons in 1871.

THE CURATORS

The first library statutes in 1610 had specified there should be eight Bodleian curators, a governing body of University men, including the vice chancellor of the University, both proctors and five professors. One of the roles of these curators was to visit the Library once a year on 8 November, the anniversary of its founding, to check the condition of the Library and stocktake. By 1615 the curators were each given a copy of the statutes, a list of the books on the shelves and a catalogue of all the best new books from Frankfurt. The curators are still responsible for overseeing the University libraries and ensuring they meet the needs of scholars and academics alike. Today there are eighteen curators, working to ensure the Bodleian remains one of the foremost scholarly libraries in the world.

LIBRARY FIRSTS

1601	The first ORIENTAL MANUSCRIPT in the Bodleian collection came from Sir John Fortescue in 1601, when he donated a manuscript of the book of Genesis, written in Sephardic script (used by Spanish Jews) with a Latin translation
1602	Thomas Bodley's Library first OPENED to scholars with over 2,500 books
1605	The first PRINTED CATALOGUE was produced
1620	The 1620 book catalogue was the first to ALPHABETICALLY LIST all the books by author
1749	The Radcliffe Library opened, the first CIRCULAR LIBRARY in Great Britain
1756	The first COMFORTABLE SEATING was introduced into Duke Humfrey's Library, when three dozen Windsor chairs were bought to replace the old benches
1835	Radcliffe Library printed its first CATALOGUE
1845	First HEATING SYSTEM was installed in the Old Library
1856	First UNDERGRADUATES were given access to the Library
1905	First ELECTRIC LIGHTS were installed in the Radcliffe Camera
1910	First FEMALE MEMBER of permanent staff came in 1910 when Frances Underhill was employed to work on catalogue revision
1914	The first time the NUMBER OF BOOKS in the Bodleian breached 1 million
1914	The first edition of the QUARTERLY MAGAZINE *Bodleian Quarterly Record* was published*
1919	The first INTERNAL TELEPHONE system was installed for library staff

---

* Now called *Bodleian Library Record* (BLR) and published twice a year.

1919	Bodley's Librarian Arthur Cowley bought the first newfangled TYPEWRITER for the library
1929	ELECTRIC LIGHTS were installed throughout the Library for the first time
1931	Arthur Ernest Cowley was the first Bodley's Librarian to be KNIGHTED
1937	HM Queen Mary laid the FOUNDATION stone of the New Bodleian
1946	The New Bodleian acquired the first FUMIGATION CHAMBER to deal with bookworm
1963	The library got its first PAPER CONSERVATOR, Maureen Vaisey
1988	Work on the first ONLINE CATALOGUE of books to national and international standards began
2005	The management of all University-funded libraries was first INTEGRATED in 2005 to create the largest unitary academic library system in the world
2007	Sarah Thomas became both the first WOMAN and the first AMERICAN to be made Bodley's Librarian

MOST POPULAR ELECTRONIC JOURNALS

The following electronic journals are consulted most often by Bodleian Libraries users:

JOURNAL	NO. OF DOWNLOADS (2014/15)
Nature	274,044
Science	170,510
Proceedings of the National Academy of Sciences of the USA	105,466
Journal of the American Chemical Society	69,037
Cell	65,498

BODLEIAN TREASURES:
ST DUNSTAN'S CLASSBOOK

This early manuscript (MS. Auct. F. 4. 32) contains a very special line-drawn image of St Dunstan kneeling and praying at the foot of Christ. It is likely that the picture was drawn when three of the four booklets that make up the manuscript were bound together at Glastonbury Abbey when St Dunstan himself was abbot there in the mid-tenth century. It is thought that this picture, an important example of Anglo-Saxon art, was sketched by St Dunstan himself – a Latin inscription written some centuries after the book had been bound says 'the picture and the text seen below on this page are in St Dunstan's own hand.' St Dunstan's Classbook was donated to the Library in 1601 by the mathematician and astrologer Thomas Allen (1542–1632).

THE BODLEIAN DURING THE CIVIL WAR

Oxford was the headquarters of the Royalists during the Civil War (1642–51) and many University buildings were turned over to Royalist control, including the Convocation House, which became the Court of Chancery, and the School of Natural Philosophy, which became the Court of Requests. Army supplies were housed across the Schools Quadrangle – uniforms and cloth in the Astronomy and Music rooms, provisions in Law and Logic Schools, and gunpowder and muskets in the tower.

In 1642 the Library was forced to loan the beleaguered king £500. This 'loan' was kept on the books for 140 years before finally being written off as 'bad debts'. To make matters worse the Library became cut off from London due to the conflict and so could not collect the rents from the properties it owned in Distaff Lane, meaning during this time no books could be purchased and the Librarian went unpaid. In 1646 Oxford surrendered to the Parliamentarian army. Fortunately their general, Thomas Fairfax, had a guard put on the door of the Bodleian to prevent any looting. It was this act that led to Oliver Cromwell being named as one of the benefactors of the Library on the marble donors' board. Never one to take sides, when the monarchy was restored to England in 1660 the Library spent £1 12s 6d on removing the rust from a picture of the king and rehanging it in the library.

HARDING COLLECTION

Bequeathed to the library in 1974, the Harding Collection is a vast collection of printed music, verse and drama. Walter Harding was born in South London in 1883, but his family emigrated to America and settled in Chicago when Harding was just four years old. Despite having no formal musical education, Harding made his living as a ragtime pianist and cinema organist and began to collect song books, popular music and opera scores, verse, drama and chapbooks in vast quantities. He carefully curated his collection, meticulously cataloguing his finds and storing them on home-made book-shelves at his home. Towards the end of his life Harding decided to bequeath his life's work to the Bodleian; despite never having visited Oxford, he felt somehow still connected to his country of birth. The huge collection was transported by chartered plane in 900 boxes weighing 22 tonnes. It now provides researchers at the Bodleian with one of the largest collection of seventeenth- and eighteenth-century English music and verse in the world and the largest collection of American sheet music outside North America.

BODLEIAN TREASURES:
MAGNA CARTA

Magna Carta, the great charter laying out English liberties, was sealed at Runnymede by King John in 1215. Many copies of the charter were made, each containing the king's seal, in order to be sent across the country and kept in the archives of large religious houses. The charter was so important it was reissued a number of times over the years, including in 1217 by the late King John's young son Henry III. Only four of these 1217 charters survive, three of which are housed at the Bodleian Library (the Library also has a copy of the 1225 reissue). Of the twenty-four surviving thirteenth-century copies of the charter commonly regarded as originals, five are in the Bodleian Library.

BODLEIAN LIBRARIES ONLINE

The Bodleian Library has moved with the times and like most institutions these days has a portfolio of online presences from Twitter to YouTube. A summary of the Bodleian's online and media activities (in 2014/15) are given below:

Visits to all Bodleian Libraries websites	4,223,430
Average length of website visit	2 m 45 s
Mentions on social media	136,715
Minutes watched of Bodleian YouTube channel	47,242
Twitter engagements	75,475
Facebook likes	10,303
Visits to Bodleian blogs	88,635
Mentions in international newspapers	2,216
Mentions in UK newspapers	1,397

SOME BENEFACTIONS OF NOTE

Much of the Bodleian's early collections were built on the kind gifts of generous benefactors. Some notable gifts include:

1635–40	Archbishop Laud	1,250 volumes of manuscripts
1629	Sir Thomas Roe	29 manuscripts
1629	Earl of Pembroke	Barocci Collection of 245 manuscripts
1634	Sir Kenelm Digby	238 manuscripts
1660	John Selden	8,000 books and manuscripts
1671	Thomas Lord Fairfax	129 manuscripts and 160 volumes (the Dodsworth Collection)
1678	Francis Junius	122 manuscripts
1690	Thomas Marshall	139 books and manuscripts
1735	Bishop Thomas Tanner	900 printed books and 467 manuscripts
1756	Richard Rawlinson	5,205 manuscripts, almost 2,000 books
1809	Richard Gough	3,700 volumes of maps, manuscripts and prints
1834	Francis Douce	393 manuscripts, 98 charters, 20,000 printed books, plus prints, drawings and coins
1909	Sir Chandra Shum Shere	Over 6,000 Sanskrit manuscripts
1913–22	Sir Edmund Backhouse	17,000 Chinese books and manuscripts

BANQUETS AT THE BODLEIAN

It might seem anomalous to host a banquet in a library full
of rare books, and yet over time the Bodleian has hosted a
number of feasts. Some of the most notable follow:

> On Monday 28 September 1663, *King Charles* II visited the
> library and was treated to a sumptuous banquet in Selden
> End. The confectioner's bill alone amounted to £210 10s;
> the Italian and French wines cost the University another
> £6 16s.

> In 1687 another banquet was held in Selden End, this
> time for *King James* II. The feast included 111 dishes in
> total, including 28 dishes of sweetmeats, 28 dishes of
> cold meat and fish, plus bowls piled high with fruit,
> and hot dishes of quail, partridge, mutton and pheasant.
> James II did not invite anyone to sup with him, but
> conversed with the fifth Librarian Dr Thomas Hyde
> on Chinese religion while he modestly picked at the
> food. Once the king had left, the staff and scholars at
> the Bodleian rushed at the laden table and scoffed the
> remaining food in a most unseemly fashion.

> In 1814 a stupendous banquet was held at the Radcliffe
> Camera in honour of the *Allied Sovereigns* and to celebrate
> their recent victories over Napoleon. This extraordinary
> event was presided over by the Prince Regent with no
> less than the King of Prussia and the Tsar of Russia in
> attendance. The tsar stayed at Merton College while he
> was in Oxford and legend has it that he found the bed
> in his room so uncomfortable that he slept on the floor.
> The large circular table on which the banquet was held
> turned up at auction in San Francisco almost 200 years
> later.

On 5 July 1988 a grand banquet was held in the Radcliffe Camera with the *Prince of Wales* as guest of honour to celebrate the 500th anniversary of Duke Humfrey's library and to launch a major new fundraising campaign. The 245 guests enjoyed a sunny evening (and so fortunately the 200 specially ordered black and white Bodleian umbrellas were not needed – these were later sold in the Bodleian shop). To celebrate the special event Prince Charles was presented with a silver reader's card.

STAFF NUMBERS

When the library statutes were enshrined in 1610 there was provision for just three staff – a librarian, a sub-librarian and a janitor. As the library grew, so too did its staff. Today the library employs 546 people across thirty libraries. The growth in staffing is laid out below:

YEAR	STAFF
1610	3
1695	4
1845	9
1882	18
1911	21
1916	68
1927	62
1938	107
1951	147
1963	226
1996	502
2015	546

BODLEIAN TREASURES:
WIND OF CHANGE SPEECH

The Bodleian holds a number of British prime ministers' papers (see p. 5). One of the treasures of Harold Macmillan's papers is the original draft of his now famous 'Wind of Change' speech (MS. Macmillan dep. c. 788, fol. 155r). Macmillan delivered the speech to both houses of the South African parliament on 3 February 1960; his powerful words immediately created headlines around the world. Macmillan had already delivered the speech earlier in his African tour at Accra in Nigeria, but that version did not include the famous line 'The wind of change is blowing throughout the continent', which elevated the speech to a new level. The Bodleian's copy includes Macmillan's copious handwritten notes and corrections, revealing the development of the typed-out speech, the famous line seemingly an afterthought added in pencil.

LAUDIAN COLLECTION

William Laud (1573–1645), Archbishop of Canterbury and Chancellor of Oxford University, was also a keen collector of ancient manuscripts. A powerful voice in the Church and ally of King Charles I, he embraced High Church ritual and aimed to enforce uniformity of worship across England. But as the power of Parliament grew in a precursor to Civil War, Laud's star began to wane. Between 1635 and 1640 (just before he was imprisoned for treason) Laud donated 1,300 manuscripts to the Bodleian, almost doubling its holdings. Many of the manuscripts were Persian, Turkish or in Arabic, making the Bodleian a centre for oriental studies. Laud made it the condition of gift that none of the manuscripts he donated could leave the Library, except to go to the University press for printing. In 1645, Laud was beheaded at Tower Hill.

COLLECTION OF CURIOSITIES

Before the foundation of the Ashmolean Museum, the Bodleian served as the home of Oxford's many collections, including its many paintings, natural history specimens, coins, medals and curios. Some of the collection's curiosities included:

Guy Fawkes' lantern, presented to the Library in 1641 by Robert Heywood of Brasenose College, whose father had arrested the infamous plotter in the cellars under the Houses of Parliament in 1605.

A crocodile from Jamaica, which was given in 1658 by Major-General John Desborough. In 1671 the Library had a case made for the crocodile for 12 shillings.

In 1678 the storekeeper at Deptford Dockyard, John Davies, gave a chair fashioned from the timbers of Sir Francis Drake's ship 'The Golden Hind'.

Also in 1678 the Library paid 15 shillings for the skeleton of a whale, gifted by apothecary William Jordan, to be transported from Lechlade to Oxford.

There were also a number of botanical and zoological specimens such as the 'trash out of the stomach of an ostrich', a salamander, a basilisk, a radish root in the shape of a hand, a Roman battleaxe and a mermaid's hand.

As Oxford was a Royalist stronghold during the Civil War (1642–51), a number of curious Royalist objects were later included in the collection, such as a cup made from a walnut tree, the fruit of which had been used to blacken King Charles II's face and hands when he was disguising himself to make his escape after defeat the Battle of Worcester, and a salver made from the 'royal oak' tree in which Charles II hid.

In 1894, included in the gift of many of Percy and Mary Shelley's letters, notebooks and relics was *a locket containing locks of both Percy and Mary Shelley's hair*. The Bodleian has a large collection of Shelley objects, including a guitar Shelley bought for Jane Williams. It is still in very good condition and is said to have not been played since Shelley's death. It was gifted to the Bodleian in 1898.

A rather more surprising item is *a locket once gifted to Lord Byron*. The story goes that the locket was sent by his married lover Lady Caroline Lamb and contains a lock of her pubic hair.

THE DOUCE COLLECTION

One of the most important bequests to the Library came in 1834 when the collection of antiquarian Francis Douce (1757–1834) arrived at the Bodleian. The amazing collection includes 44,000 prints, 20,000 books, 1,500 drawings and 430 manuscripts. Douce left something of a joke in his will when he bequeathed a box to the British Museum with instructions that it should not be opened until 1 January 1900. Interest was piqued as to what Douce might have left the great institution, especially considering he had worked there himself for a short period of time and had resigned, submitting a letter of complaint with fourteen reasons why he was leaving, including 'The want of society with the members, their habits wholly different & their manners far from fascinating & sometimes repulsive.' The British Museum kept its word and the box remained untouched until 1900, when the trustees gathered to open it. Reports of the exact contents of the box differ (some say it was nothing but rubbish, others report it was many old notebooks and book covers), but it seems the trustees felt it was of no value and in 1930 the box was sent to the Bodleian to join the rest of the Douce collection.

BODLEY BOYS

When faced with the problem of a chronic lack of both staff and funds, in 1883 the thirteenth Bodley's Librarian E.W.B. Nicholson introduced the idea of employing local boys. Boys aged between fourteen and eighteen years were employed on an apprenticeship basis, with general education and lectures on librarianship making up an important part of their time at the Library (Nicholson also insisted that all the boys learned to swim after one unfortunate boy drowned in the River Cherwell). The younger (and lower paid) boys were tasked with fetching books, and the older boys with returning the books. Each year a prize of £2 and 2 shillings was awarded to the 'most deserving boy'. The winner could choose books subject to the Librarian's approval, but they were strongly advised to select Liddell & Scott's *Greek Lexicon* and Lewis & Short's *Latin Dictionary*.

The *Staff-Kalendar* of 1904 lists the 'Regulations Relating to Boys'. Boys would be supplied with a special duster for cleaning dirty books. Boys with colds and coughs were expected to come to work, but were stationed 'out of draughts and changes of temperature'. Boys should be careful of straining themselves by carrying too many books at once. Half-day holidays would be awarded for making good suggestions. The scheme was a great success and fulfilled Nicholson's aim of creating a kind of unofficial librarian training school, giving many people a start in the library world. Various Bodley Boys went on to be chief librarians of the National Central Library, the London Library, Chetham's Library in Manchester and the university libraries of Sheffield and Melbourne, to name a few. The Bodley Boys scheme, which later came to include girls as well, ended in the 1950s but the tradition continued in the form of employing young people to work in the bookstack, many of whom went on to have long and successful careers elsewhere in the Bodleian and other libraries.

THE RADCLIFFE CAMERA

In 1714 notable physician John Radcliffe bequeathed £40,000 in his will for the building of a new library* in Oxford. Two architects submitted plans: James Gibbs and Nicholas Hawksmoor. Hawksmoor favoured a bold round design and was asked to create a wooden scale model, which still survives in the Bodleian's collection today; Gibbs designed a more conventional rectangular building. Hawksmoor's design was favoured but unfortunately he died in 1736 before building had commenced, so Gibbs was offered the commission. Gibbs abandoned his rectangular design and adapted Hawksmoor's original design to create the now iconic domed building – the first circular library of its kind in Britain. Some facts relating to the original Radcliffe Library are laid out below:

Foundation stone laid	1737
Architect	James Gibbs
Opened	1749
Type of stone	limestone from Headington and Burford stone
Roof construction	timber with 63 tonnes of Derbyshire lead
First catalogue	1835
First librarian	Francis Wise
Incorporated into Bodleian	1860
First book in the collection	Thomas Carte's *A General History of England*
First bequest	50,000 pamphlets in 1749 from Mr Bartholomew of University College

---

* There was a plan for the Radcliffe Library to be built at the west end of Selden End, part of the Old Library, but because the building would have covered over some of the gardens of Exeter College the Fellows there demanded a large amount of compensation. As a result the scheme was abandoned and the new location between School Street and Catte Street was agreed.

The Radcliffe Library was initially poorly attended, its books seeming a sideline to the wondrous building itself. Radcliffe had provided £100 a year for new books but this fund was controlled by the trustees rather than the librarian so initial acquisitions were slow. From c. 1810 the library became a specialized scientific library under librarian George Williams. In 1860 the Radcliffe Library was incorporated into the Bodleian, the majority of its collection moved to the new University Museum (and later still to a dedicated Science Library on Parks Road), and it was renamed the Radcliffe Camera. In 1862 it reopened as a reading room for the Bodleian (although its first day was a bit of a disappointment as not one reader showed up). However, since then its popularity has grown and it has become the main reading room for History and English Literature undergraduates. Below are some key facts about the Radcliffe Camera today:

Number of desks	300
Number of reading rooms	3
Bookstore under Radcliffe square excavated*	1909–12
Number of books held when bookstore in use	600,000
Gladstone link opened as open-stack space	2011
(see p. 89)	

(see p. 89)

THE TANNER COLLECTION

Thomas Tanner (1674–1735) was an avid collector of books and manuscripts. He was appointed canon of Christ Church in 1724 and decided to move his book collection from his home in Norwich to Oxford. Tanner hired a barge to take the books down the river in 1731 but unfortunately disaster struck near Wallingford when the boat sank. Many of the books were rescued from the river and to this day bear the marks

---

* When the underground bookstack was excavated, it was designed to hold approx. 1,000,000 8° books (however it only ever actually held 600,000).

from the water damage they suffered. In 1735 Tanner died and bequeathed his library of 900 volumes to the Bodleian. His collection included a copy of the Bay Psalm Book from 1640 – the first book to be printed in North America (see p. 31). The Tanner manuscripts included many letters from the most important historical figures during the Civil War years, including Charles I, Oliver Cromwell, Prince Rupert and John Hampden. The manuscripts were sorted and bound into 467 volumes.

THE BODLEIAN DURING WORLD WAR I

In January 1916, 16 members of a staff of 68 were serving in the army; a year later this rose to 22, and to 30 by February 1917. Two members of staff, Lieutenant R.A. Abrams and Lieutenant H.J. Dunn, were killed during the conflict; they were both just twenty-eight years old.* Senior sub-librarian Arthur Cowley volunteered to work for the Red Cross ambulance service in France as he was too old for active service, so was also away from the Library, as was junior sub-librarian (and later the sixteenth Bodley's Librarian) Edmund Craster, who saw active service. As the staff of the Library became sucked into the war, so too did many academics and students, and the Library became rather quieter than usual (although the fourteenth Bodley's Librarian Falconer Madan commented that women students remained numerous). It was feared that Oxford might be bombed, so many of the most valuable manuscripts and books were moved to the south-west corner of the underground bookstore and surrounded by a wall of sandbags. Fortunately, although Zeppelins passed overhead a number of times, Oxford and the Bodleian remained safe.

---

* A memorial to all the 139 librarians killed in the First World War was erected in 1924 at the British Museum.

FRIENDS OF THE BODLEIAN

In 1925 Sir Michael Sadler helped to set up Friends of the Bodleian, with the aim of helping the Bodleian to purchase more books – the first such organization for any library in the world. Thanks to the Friends many first editions of works by luminaries such as Keats, Coleridge, Wordsworth, Smollett, Swift and Pope were added to the collection. Contemporary authors also donated their works to the Library, including Walter de la Mare, who gave a draft of *The Memoirs of a Midget*; T.S. Eliot, who donated manuscripts of 'The Rock' and 'Marina'; and Gustav Holst, who gave a vocal score of 'A Choral Fantasia'. This creation of Friends proved so successful that further international groups were set up: Bodley's American Friends in 1957, Canadian Friends in 1983, German Friends in 1988, Japanese Friends in 1990 and South American Friends in 1994.

BODLEIAN TREASURES:
PLINY'S *NATURALIS HISTORIA*

Pliny's (23–79 CE) *Naturalis Historia* (*Natural History*) was a groundbreaking book of its time, comprising a history of the natural world. The work contains thirty-seven books organized into ten volumes. Covering everything from astronomy, through botany to anthropology, it represents a fascinating insight into the Roman understanding of the natural world. The Bodleian's most famous copy (Arch. G b.6) is from 1476 and was lavishly produced on vellum for the Strozzi family of Florence. It was printed by the great Venetian printer Nicolas Jenson and incorporates many highly illuminated illustrations.

THE NEW BODLEIAN

By the 1920s the Library was at full capacity and new space was desperately needed to allow the collection to continue to grow. So in 1931 the building of a new library was proposed and, thanks to a large grant from the Rockefeller Foundation, a location on Broad Street was secured. Sir Giles Gilbert Scott, who had already designed Cambridge University Library and the now iconic red telephone box, was enlisted in 1934 to design the ambitious New Bodleian. The New Bodleian was effectively a huge storehouse for books and owed much of its design to the Sterling Library at Yale. The bookstack was partially sunk into the ground to reduce the height of the building. A tunnel underneath Broad Street was built to connect the old and new libraries; it contained a conveyer (see p. 95) to transport books and a pneumatic Lamson tube system* for book requests. Some key facts relating to the New Bodleian:

Number of books in bookstack	3.5 million
Height of bookstack	11 floors†
Bookstack made of	steel
Number of floors of bookstack below ground	3
Height of each floor	2 metres
Number of years the New Bodleian served its readers	70‡

---

* Pneumatic tube systems were popular in the late nineteenth century in shops, banks and libraries. They employed a series of tubes which used pneumatic compressed air to suck small items along the tube. This efficient system meant messages, reader requests or small amounts of money could be quickly transported between floors.

† When excavating the bookstack for the New Bodleian, once the diggers reached the last 30 cm of gravel suddenly water began to pour into the hole at a rate of 9,000–14,000 litres an hour. Luckily there was a plan in place to line the site with interlocking steel sheet piling, which prevented the water getting in.

‡ When the New Bodleian was officially opened by King George VI on 24 October 1946, the ornate silver ceremonial key broke in the lock of the door. Much pushing and pulling followed, but the door would not give. Fortunately, the nimble Bedel of Arts, Mr G.W. Beesley, was able to get his fingers onto the shank of the broken key and turn it, and the doors were finally opened.

In 2010–14 the New Bodleian underwent an ambitious remodelling and was renamed the Weston Library. The following statistics reveal the extent of the rebuilding work:

Amount of concrete used	6,500 tonnes
Amount of asbestos removed from building	80 tonnes
Amount of steel removed	1,000 tonnes
Amount of general waste removed	260 tonnes
Amount of shelving removed from stacks	81 km
Amount of shelving removed from reading rooms and offices	3 km
Number of worker hours	Over 1 million
Length of demolition phase	12 months
Size of crane	120 foot high
Number of original aluminium windows refurbished	200
Amount of flooring screed laid	3,000 sq. m.

BOOK CLASSIFICATION

When the library was first established in the seventeenth century the books were organized by faculty: theology, jurisprudence, medicine and then arts. Within these sections, books were divided according to size and then arranged alphabetically by the author's name. Manuscripts were shelved in among them. Lists or tables were then stuck to each end of the bookcases, listing in shelf order the books in that particular case. The first Librarian, Thomas James, sent copies of these book lists regularly to Thomas Bodley so that he could use them when acquiring new books to make sure he was not buying duplicates.

This method of classifying the books by subject broke down over time as librarians could not agree over which books went in which subject and how the subjects were subdivided (initially mathematics was somewhat randomly classified as an arts subject). Books then began to be classified by size, as a book's location was dependent on the size of the shelf. But into the eighteenth and nineteenth centuries, as the Library gained more space, books became more commonly classified by their location (so an item stored in a cupboard in Duke Humfrey's Library would have a shelfmark starting Arch., for 'Archivium').

In 1856 the subject of classification came up again, and it was suggested that some kind of subject ordering was necessary, especially as the collection grew larger. The twelfth Librarian, Henry Coxe, was sent off to the British Museum and Cambridge University Library to see how they were doing things. Again it was the British Museum, with its system of 'relative location' (where the books are numbered according to each other rather than to the shelf), that was to be the inspiration for the new arrangement adopted for acquisitions to the Library after that.

From 1861, when the Radcliffe Camera became part of the Bodleian, Henry Coxe decided that all books in the Camera should be placed in classified order: this was possible as only modern books were to be shelved there. This new, more ordered system was once again based on classification by subject.

By 1864 Coxe realized he could not reclassify all the books in the Bodleian so instead focused on unclassified additions to the Library since 1824. This scheme of subject classification developed by Coxe took the original nine classes of subject up to seventy-three subdivisions of these subjects.

Coxe's successor as the thirteenth Bodley's Librarian, E.W.B. Nicholson, took Coxe's subject classification even further and expanded the subjects to include, among others, social and political science. Nicholson's vastly more rigorous subject classification system has over 7,000 subjects and subdivisions, including Ecclesiastical history – the conflict with imperial paganism (incl. Acts of Martyrs); Armorial bearings – war cries, party cries; Writing and Illumination – specimens of autographs and autograph collecting. These were further subdivided into books, periodicals, serials, directories and newspapers, and also into seven sizes.

Since 1988, when the electronic catalogue was introduced, the Nicholson system of classification has been closed.

JOHN JOHNSON COLLECTION
OF PRINTED EPHEMERA

Transferred from the Oxford University Press to the Bodleian, in 1968, the John Johnson Collection of Printed Ephemera filled two rooms in the New Bodleian. The collection was assembled by John de Monins Johnson (1882–1956), Printer to the University from 1925 to 1946. Johnson started to collect common printed items (which would usually have been thrown away), such as leaflets, adverts, menus, postcards and programmes, retrospectively in the 1930s, in order to document developments in printing and in social history. The collection consists of over 1.5 million printed items and is considered one of the most important collections of printed ephemera in the world. Some highlights include playbills printed on silk, elaborate valentines, trade cards and advertisements. Now back in the Weston Library, the collection is of huge value to those studying British social history from the eighteenth century onwards. The earliest item of ephemera in the collection is from 1508, but the majority of the ephemera are from the eighteenth, nineteenth and early twentieth centuries. Recently 67,754 items from the collection were scanned and made available for study online through the ProQuest project The John Johnson Collection: an Archive of Printed Ephemera.

In 2006 Wilkinson Eyre architects were selected to oversee the refurbishment of the New Bodleian into the Weston Library (so named because of a generous £25 million gift from the Garfield Weston Foundation). Because of the vast new Book Storage Facility in Swindon fewer books needed to be stored at the New Bodleian; this gave scope for opening up the space occupied by the massive bookstack and redeveloping the Library as a special collections research library, with conservation studios and exhibition galleries for the Library's treasures. Some key facts about the Weston Library are below:

Cost of redevelopment	£80 million
Number of reading rooms	3
The first book to be shelved in the Weston	Plato's complete works in Greek
Official opening	March 2015
Number of seats in lecture theatre	119
Number of exhibition galleries	2
Size of open-shelf galleries	2.5 km
No. of volumes in open-shelf	85,000
No. of study spaces	285
No. of visitors to Blackwell Hall in first year of opening	773,299

When the New Bodleian Library was opened in 1946, the bells of All Saints Church (now Lincoln College Library) were rung in a special peal to commemorate the event. So at 3 p.m. on Saturday 21 March 2015 the Church bells were rung again by the Oxford Society of Change Ringers to mark the reopening of the New Bodleian as the Weston Library. The New Bodleian was built from Bladon and Clipsham limestone, with the interior veneer from Taynton stone. Unfortunately the Taynton quarry is now closed, so when refurbishing the interior very similar Creeton limestone was sourced from Lincolnshire. As with the original Taynton stone, it was given a wash of tea in order to bring out the colour of the stone.

THE BODLEIAN IN WORLD WAR II

During World War II, as books were transferred into the vast bookstacks of the New Bodleian, a number of treasures were deposited in the new building for safe keeping while the war raged. Many of the colleges transferred their precious books, but alongside these came other special objects such as the medieval glass from New College Chapel, type plates from the Clarendon Press, paintings from the Christ Church picture gallery and seeds from the botany department. Below is a list of some of the institutions that sent their books and archives for safe keeping at the New Bodleian for the duration of the war:

London School of Economics | Science Museum
Natural History Museum | Eton College
University of London Library | British Drama League
Oxford & Cambridge Club | Royal Society
Mineralogical Society | Linnaean Society | British Museum
House of Parliament | House of Lords
Royal Statistical Society | Geological Society
Victoria & Albert Museum | Royal Geographical Society
General Register Office at Somerset House

Due to the immense value (both culturally and monetarily) the library needed to be well protected in the event of a bombing raid: thus from 1942 it became the norm for thirty people trained as firefighters to be on duty overnight, every night in the library.

VETERA SHELFMARKS

The following system with shelfmarks starting Vet. (short for *vetera*, from *vetus* meaning 'old') was introduced in 1937 for antiquarian accessions; it can reveal the country of printing, the period it was written in and the size of the book by the number and letter codes listed in the shelfmark. There are believed to be over 35,000 volumes with a Vet. shelfmark.

An explanation of the codes used is as follows. Given the code Vet. A5 f.3877 as an example, Vet. reveals it is a vetera shelfmark; A is the country code; 5 is the period classification; f. is the volume size; 3877 is the running number.

COUNTRY CODES

A	GB and Ireland
B	Netherlands and Belgium
C	Denmark, Norway, Sweden, Iceland
D	Germany, Austria, Switzerland
E	France
F	Italy
G	Spain and Portugal
H	Russia, Poland and Hungary
I	Rest of Europe
K	North America
KK	Rest of the world
L	Unknown
M	General collections, for books where items come from different countries

PERIOD CLASSIFICATION

1.	1501–1600
2.	1601–1640
3.	1641–1700
4.	1701–1750
5.	1751–1800
6.	1801–1850
7.	1851–1900

BOOK SIZES

The Library employed two book-sizing systems: the one below used lower-case letters to indicate the sizing; the other, developed by thirteenth Bodley's Librarian E.W.B. Nicholson, used upper-case letters – the only key difference being the largest book size, which under Nicholson's system A included books over 18 inches in height. The lower-case book sizing system is as follows:

a	over 20 inches
b	15–20 inches
c	12–15 inches
d	9–12 inches
e	7–9 inches
f	5–7 inches
g	under 5 inches

E is the most common size for modern books, followed by F then D.

BODLEIAN CHAIR

In 1756 the twenty-eight curators of the Bodleian Library bought three dozen Windsor chairs of comb-back elbow style. In 1936 Gilbert Scott designed two new styles of readers' chairs for the New Bodleian – one bucket-style, one straight-backed, both clad in leather – sixty of which have survived and were refurbished for the reopening of the Weston Library. To celebrate the opening of the Weston Library a competition was launched to design a new readers' chair. The chair needed to both stylish and functional – readers would expect to sit studying on the chairs for many hours, and they needed to be silent to use. Sixty entries were received, which were whittled down to six teams, and then just three designs were made into prototype chairs to be tested by readers. In September 2013 an elegant oak three-legged chair designed by Edward Barber and Jay Osgerby and manufactured by Isokon Plus was named the winner.

PHI COLLECTION

The thirteenth Bodley's Librarian E.W.B. Nicholson introduced the Φ or Phi collection for obscene or libellous works. No one knows for sure why it was named thus. Some suggest it was a pun on the word 'fie!', which a librarian might exclaim in disapproval when asked to fetch one such book; others postulate that it stems from the first letter 'phi' of the Greek *phaula* or *phaulos*, standing for worthless, wicked or base. By 1912 the system had been formalized to the extent that undergraduates had to secure written permission from a tutor in order to consult anything in the Phi collection and no boys (the young men employed to retrieve books) were allowed to fetch anything in the collection. In 1937 the Phi collection was said to be divided into three categories: works of sexual pathology or physiology whose illustrations or candour made them unsuitable for general access; obscene literature; and nude drawings or photos which could inspire pornographic interest. The librarians were fairly strict about allowing access to the Phi collection and many request slips survive in the archives detailing cases in which the librarian had to be persuaded by tutors that a student's request was genuine. By the late 1930s much of the Phi material was reclassified and redistributed into the collection, but the shelfmark was not retired and still persists today (for example for copies of the pornographic magazine *Razzle* (Phi d.311)). Some of the titles that found their way into the Phi collection over the years include:

The Works of the Earls of Rochester, Roscommon, and Dorset
    by J.W. Rochester (1731)
Studies in the Psychology of Sex (1897–1910) by Havelock Ellis
Ulysses (1922) by James Joyce
Geschicte der erotschen Kunst (1908) by Edmund Fuchs
Sleeveless Errand (1929) by Norah C. James
Lady Chatterley's Lover (1928) by D.H. Lawrence
25 Nudes (1938) by Eric Gill
Sex (1992) by Madonna

Other libraries had a similar system for classifying obscene material. In Cambridge University Library it was given an 'Arc' (Arcana) shelfmark, and the British Library kept all such books in a special 'private case'.

FIRST FEMALE EMPLOYEE

E.W.B. Nicholson, the thirteenth Bodley's Librarian from 1881 to 1912, was responsible for introducing female employees to the Bodleian staff roll, but it was not an easy process. In the early years of the twentieth century there were a few women, including Nicholson's own daughters Myrtle and May, who occasionally helped out in the Library as volunteers. Nicholson, an enlightened man who was a lifelong champion of women's rights, saw the opportunity to put forward this cause and solve a major staffing problem at the same time. In 1910 Nicholson told the curators of the Bodleian that he would like to hire Frances Underhill, who had been doing excellent work as a part-time employee, as a permanent assistant and pay her £154 per year. The curators were horrified by such a suggestion and referred the matter to a subcommittee. So began the long and painful process of discussing whether women were capable of doing the job of assistant and what the effects would be of letting them loose in the library as proper employees. Letters were written to all the other great libraries in the country to discover their views on the matter. Only one library replied, saying that they had already taken this daring course of action – William K. Dickson of the Advocates Library in Edinburgh wrote back singing the praises of a certain Miss Barclay who had been working for him since 1906. The committee also asked current employees of the Bodleian for their views, and a list was compiled of the tasks they thought women would not be capable of. These included:

Climbing ladders | taking responsible messages
carrying books | being in charge of other people

72

One assistant, Strickland Gibson, did not agree with this and came out in support of Nicholson, pointing out that women already managed to go up the ladders without causing any problems. Nicholson then wrote a letter to the curators in which he systematically refuted the list of objections. It worked, and on 29 October 1910 Frances Underhill's nomination was passed by five votes to four. The Bodleian Library had its first female assistant.

CLOSING ROUTINE

In 1604 Thomas Bodley provided the first Librarian, Thomas James, with a bell that was to be rung each night to indicate that the Library was about to close. Since then the closing routine has grown somewhat more complex. Below is a summary of the current closing routine:

45 minutes before	No access to the Gladstone link from the Lower Camera or Bodleian.
30 minutes before	Photocopiers turned off and no further staff-service photocopy orders will be taken. All windows closed. Bookcase lights turned off.
15 minutes before	All reader computers turned off.
10 minutes before	A bell is rung to signal the imminent closure of the building.
5 minutes before	Main lights turned off.

DUKE HUMFREY'S NIGHT

Duke Humfrey's night, a benefit event held by the Friends of
the Bodleian (see p. 62), raises much-needed funds for the
purchase and conservation of items in special collections. First
organized in 2010, it is held in October, as close as possible to
the birthday of early benefactor Humfrey, Duke of Gloucester.
Around fifty items from special collections are displayed in
Duke Humfrey's Library; visitors can donate sums of money
for their purchase or conservation. In return a bookplate
in the sponsored item will forever record the name of an
individual or institution, or a dedication to a loved one.

IMPRESSIONS OF THE
NINETEENTH-CENTURY BODLEIAN

Travels through England, Wales, & Scotland, in the year 1816 by Samuel
Heinrich Spiker contains the following impression of the
Bodleian Library as it was in the early nineteenth century:

> The Bodleian Library consist of three apartments, which
> run into one another in such a manner as nearly to
> resemble a lying 'H'. They are but poorly lighted by
> the large arched window next the entrance, and the
> lowness of the rooms contributes to render them still
> more gloomy. The dark colour of the wood too, of
> which the cases are made, gives the whole a very sombre
> appearance. A gallery of no great height, filled with
> book-cases, is allowed to be entered by the librarians
> only. The printed catalogues of the Bodleian Library, lie
> for inspection on a desk near the window; the books are
> contained in four volumes, and the manuscripts in two.
> Both catalogues are interleaved with blank paper, for the
> purpose of entering in them the new books which are
> from time to time added to the library.

DIGITIZATION

The Oxford Digital Library Project was launched in 2000 with the aim of digitizing important, unique or ancient books in the collection. Working with partner Google between 2004 and 2009, over 300,000 out-of-copyright and out-of-print books have been made available online as part of the Google Book Project. Since then the Library has worked with a number of other partners, including the Vatican Library (Biblioteca Apostolica Vaticana or BAV), with whom they have been digitizing and making available online a number of Hebrew and Greek texts from across their collections. In 2014/15 a total of 251,964 pages were digitized in the studio at the Weston Library.

ARTEFACTS FOUND DURING
NEW BODLEIAN DEMOLITION

During the demolition and remodelling of the New Bodleian/ Weston Library, builders found the following items:

* WD & HO Wills' 'Capstan' Navy Cut cigarette packet
* Smiths 'Quality' Californian Raisins packet
* John Wiblin's Royal Oxford sausages paper bag
* George VI pale red-brown 1½d stamp
* 'Imp' soap paper bag
* Californian Poppy perfume card
* Lovell's Liquorice Toffee Rex sweet wrapper
* High Speed Twist Drill Bits paper packet containing seven drill bits
* Vernons football pools coupons for 4 September 1954
* Handwritten note containing address of POW camp in Italy
* Receipt from Blackwell's for book purchased by Red Cross POW on 23 June 1942

When the New Bodleian was being built in 1936 careful note was taken of any objects uncovered, as the diggers excavated the area in what became one of the first urban 'rescue investigations', now common practice in commercial archaeology. Three mammoth teeth were unearthed, as was a huge amount of medieval pottery.

THE BODLEIAN PIN COLLECTION

There are many strange things in the Bodleian Library, but one of the most unexpected is surely the collection of pins that were taken out of manuscripts and books in the nineteenth century. Before the invention of the paper clip, the stapler and household glue, the humble pin was a truly invaluable object. Its uses were not restricted to sewing as they are today, and it was used to hold all manner of things together, including papers. In the late nineteenth century the *Summary Catalogue of Western Manuscripts* was being compiled and during this arduous process a large number of pins were removed from the books and manuscripts being sorted. The librarians' characteristic need to preserve and record soon took over and instead of simply throwing the pins away, they began to attach them to small pieces of paper and record any information available about them: their age, the title and date of the book they were found in, and so on. The earliest examples in the collection are from the early seventeenth century, but it is interesting to note that the design and construction of pins did not change between the sixteenth and mid-nineteenth centuries, when a pin-making machine came into production.

In 2011 the Bodleian pin collection received a distinguished addition: a pin that had belonged to none other than Jane Austen. She had used it, and two others that were subsequently lost, to edit her manuscript of *The Watsons* by adding new paragraphs on separate pieces of paper. This early, lo-fi example of cut-and-paste was documented by the famous Austen editor R.W. Chapman. He removed the three pins from the manuscript because he was concerned they would erode and damage the paper. Other pins have been found in Austen manuscripts and they are all the same: handmade, two-piece tinned brass with applied wound-wire heads. However, they are slightly shorter than sewing pins, which suggests that they might have been especially designed for other purposes. These pins provide us with a fascinating insight into how Jane Austen wrote and edited her texts, and along with the others in the Bodleian pin collection are quirky examples of bibliographic ephemera.

SOME SHELFMARKS OF NOTE

res. was the mostly heavily restricted of the Bodleian's shelfmarks, used for works which readers could not be legally permitted to access because of libel, sedition or simply because the publisher had withdrawn the book from circulation. It also covers D notices and items which come under the thirty-year rule (i.e. government papers not to be viewed by the public until thirty years have passed).

Cons. Res. is a location shelfmark for vulnerable and or very fragile manuscripts awaiting conservation, and therefore withdrawn from use in the meantime. Those items that are repaired in the conservation studio can then be returned to use under their normal shelfmarks.

Arch. Bodl. D was used as a secondary Phi (Φ) collection (see p. 71) for obscene material. It has now been closed and all the items reclassified.

sub fen This shelfmark was created to show the location of certain books, sub fen. being short for *sub fenestra*, meaning the items were kept below the window in the Auctarium (anatomy school).

Bicycles	The John Johnson Collection of Ephemera (see p. 66) has a number of quirky shelfmarks including 'bicycle', under which ephemera relating to bicycles (such as bike adverts) are classified. Other interesting shelfmarks from this collection include: circus, soap, ironmongery, beauty parlour and patent medicines.
Shelley relics	A shelfmark relating to the many objects in the Bodleian's extensive collection of items belonging to or related to Percy Bysshe Shelley, such as his baby rattle and his spyglass.
Arch.	Books which due to their value, very small size or rarity would not be suitably placed in the usual system of classification; for example, volumes with early photographs included would be under this shelfmark.
Don.	Books donated to the library 1925–82 through Friends of the Bodleian, American Friends or directly donated.

INCUNABULA

Incunabula are early printed (not handwritten) books or pamphlets produced in Europe between 1450 and 1500. The term was first coined by bibliophile Bernhard von Mallinckrodt in his 1639 pamphlet *De ortu et progressu artis typographicae* (Of the rise and progress of the typographic art). Mallinckrodt defined incunabula (which roughly translates as 'from the cradle') as books printed up to 1500. Books printed after 1500 are known as post-incunabula. There are roughly 30,000 known editions of incunabula, most surviving in multiple copies, with over one-third of all known incunabula held in Germany. The Bodleian has over 5,600 incunabula, the largest collection in a university library and the fifth largest collection of any library in the world (the British Library holds the largest).

THE LIBRARY TODAY IN NUMBERS

There are currently more than 12 million printed items in the libraries' collections, over 1 million electronic books and huge quantities of other material. With around 250,000 printed items added to the Library in 2014/15 the collection is ever growing. A snapshot of the Bodleian today is provided by these figures from 31 July 2014:

Total catalogued printed stock	11,910,646
Electronic books	1,064,063
Linear metres of manuscripts and archives	25,583
Members of staff	546
Maps in the collection	1.25 million
Total number of libraries (excluding separate stores)	30
Study spaces	4,071
Open access computers	513
Total number of registered users	64,242
Number of registered external users	32,053
Items in the Book Storage Facility	9,503,788

BODLEIAN TREASURES: HANDEL'S *MESSIAH*

The 'conducting score' of George Frideric Handel's famous oratorio *Messiah* (MSS. Tenbury 346–7) is one of the great treasures of the Bodleian's music collection. After he had finished composing the work, Handel commissioned John Christopher Smith (the elder) to make a neat copy of his original manuscript, and it was this score which he used to direct the first performances in Dublin in 1742 and all subsequent performances until his sight failed. The composer annotated the score with performance instructions and the names of singers at various performances. He also inserted new versions of some of the arias in his own hand. In the nineteenth century the manuscript was given to Sir Frederick Ouseley, Heather Professor of Music at Oxford, whose collection became the basis of the library of St Michael's College, Tenbury Wells, which Ouseley founded in 1856. When the College closed down in 1985, the majority of the collection came to the Bodleian.

THE TOWER OF THE FIVE ORDERS

The Tower of the Five Orders, built between 1613 and 1619, stands in the Schools Quadrangle. It is so named because it features columns from each of the five orders of classical architecture, as follows:

TUSCAN | DORIC | IONIC | CORINTHIAN | COMPOSITE

In very simple terms, Tuscan columns are plain without ornament; Doric columns are relatively stout and plain; Ionic are the thinnest and smallest of the columns and have volutes (a scroll-shaped ornament); Corinthian are slender, fluted columns with a great deal of ornamentation; and Composite columns have a mixture of the Ionic volutes and the Corinthian ornamentation.

THE PICTURE GALLERY

When the Bodleian Library was founded there was no public museum in Oxford, so it soon became a repository not just for books but also for paintings, coins, natural history specimens and curios (see p. 56), many of which were moved to the Ashmolean Museum when it opened in 1845. The Upper Reading Room on the second floor of the Schools Quadrangle, built between 1613 and 1618, was initially used as a picture gallery displaying some of the many works of art in the collection at that time, such as a number of portraits of the founders of Oxford colleges. In 1830 the picture gallery was refurbished, with a new floor laid, windows blocked up to make way for further bookshelves, and the frieze painted on the ceiling panels plastered over (see p. 24). To finish off the look the bookcases and wainscoting were painted a fetching shade of green.* In 1903 the thirteenth Bodley's Librarian E.W.B. Nicholson's proposal to convert the picture gallery into a further reading room was approved. By 1907 new readers' desks and shelves of periodicals were installed and the picture gallery officially became the Upper Reading Room. Today the library still has over 400 paintings in a variety of media in its collection, but most are unfortunately no longer on display.

BODLEIAN TREASURES: BOCCACCIO'S *DECAMERON*

Lavishly illustrated, the Bodleian's finest copy of Giovanni Boccaccio's *Decameron* (MS. Holkham misc. 49) contains one of the earliest examples of Italian prose writing. The *Decameron* tells the tale of seven women and three men who, during the Black Death outbreak of 1348, met at a church in Florence and each told a story over the course of ten days. Boccaccio composed his text between 1349 and 1351; this copy was created in 1467 and was beautifully illuminated by the Renaissance artist Taddeo Crivelli, most famous for his work on the masterpiece Bible of Borso d'Este. It belonged to Thomas Coke (1697–1759), who built Holkham Hall in Norfolk. It came to the Bodleian's collection in 1981, when it was handed over by the executors of the 5th Earl of Leicester to the Treasury in lieu of tax.

---

* A watercolour of the picture gallery by Joseph Nash painted soon after the re-furbishment exists in the Library collection; it reveals the picture gallery to have been a handsome space, the walls of which were crammed with portraits.

LIBRARY SPACES

From the modest start in Duke Humfrey's Library, with scholars standing at lecterns, the number of reader spaces has grown enormously in order to meet the demands of increasing library visitors. The following statistics from 2014/15 reveal the extent of Bodleian Libraries' capacity and how it is used:

Number of libraries	30
Total gross floor area	56,340 sq. m.
Total number of study spaces	4,071
Number of open access workstations	513
Number of study spaces with audio-visual equipment	70
Number of regular opening hours per week in main library:	
Social Science Library	81 hours
Bodleian (Humanities)	77 hours
Radcliffe Science Library	79.5 hours
Cairns Library* (Medicine)	168 hours

In the last few years loans of physical books from the dependent libraries of the Bodleian in which loans are allowed have gone down, while actual visitors and users of all library spaces have gone up, suggesting a change in culture whereby people seek a collective space in which to study rather than studying alone at home.

---

* Two libraries, the Cairns and the Nuffield Orthopaedic Centre (NOC) Library, offer 24-hour opening hours.

THE BODLEY MEDAL

In 1646, the celebrated medal-maker Claude Warin designed a copper medal in honour of Sir Thomas Bodley. To celebrate the 400th anniversary of the Library's foundation it was decided that replica medals should be minted. The Royal Mint produced a new set of medals to be awarded to individuals who have made, 'outstanding contributions ... to the worlds of communication and literature' and who have helped the Library achieve 'the vision of its founder, Sir Thomas Bodley, to be a library not just to Oxford University but also to the world'. The following people are recipients of a Bodley Medal:

Tim Berners-Lee (2002) | Rupert Murdoch (2002)
P.D. James (2002) | John Warnock (2003)
Oliver Sacks (2003) | Pat Mitchell (2003)
Tom Stoppard (2004) | Seamus Heaney (2004)
Richard Attenborough (2004) | William Scheide (2005)
Helmut Friedlaender (2005) | Carl Pforzheimer III (2005)
Alan Bennett (2008) | Peter Carey (2012)
Hilary Mantel (2013) | Ian McEwan (2014)
Nicholas Hytner (2015) | Jim Eyre (2015)
Stephen Hawking (2015) | David Attenborough (2015)
Mary Beard (2016) | Maggie Smith (2016)

THE 'NO-LENDING' RULE

Ever since Thomas Bodley oversaw the running of his new library a no-lending rule has been followed. Bodley was very firm on this point as he believed the reason the previous library had failed was because the books were constantly being borrowed and not returned. To those used to borrowing books from a public library this rule can seem somewhat nonsensical, and yet it is a rule that has preserved the collection and ensures that the Bodleian remains a busy place of study. Over time the no-lending rule has been challenged a number of times.

During the English Civil War, King Charles I made Oxford his headquarters, setting up house at Christ Church, while the queen lodged at Merton. On 30 December 1645 Charles sent an order to the second Bodley's Librarian John Rouse that he wished to borrow a history of the world by Theodore Agrippa d'Aubigne. The small piece of paper with the vice chancellor's endorsement 'His Majestyes use is in commaund to us' still survives in the library's collection. Rouse hurriedly showed the king the statutes, which forbid the removal of books from the Library, and fortunately the king agreed that they ought to be adhered to.

In a repeat of history, in 1654 the Lord Protector, Oliver Cromwell, asked to borrow a manuscript from the Bodleian Library on behalf of the Portuguese ambassador. The third Bodley's Librarian, Thomas Barlow, again sent a copy of the statutes to Cromwell and refused the request. Cromwell praised the wisdom of Thomas Bodley's statutes and did not pursue the matter further.

Despite Thomas Bodley's stipulations and the precedent set by refusing to loan books to some of the most important men in England, towards the end of the seventeenth century some of the books and manuscripts from the collection were borrowed by readers. From 1679 repeated requests to return borrowed books were issued, and the practice was stopped. However, from 1856 to 1887 books from the collection began again to be loaned to senior academics and university institutions such as the Clarendon Press. This was in part due to the restricted opening hours of the Library, which meant consulting books could be awkward. This spate of lending was rooted out when the ruling body of senior staff of the University, Congregation, got wind of the informal system and stated that curators or librarians could not grant loans without the authorization of Convocation (the governing body of the University).

To this day books in the main Bodleian Library cannot be loaned out. However, many of the dependent libraries in the Bodleian Libraries group, such as the Sackler Library, do allow lending.

INSTITUTIONAL REPOSITORY

An institutional repository is a digital platform to store and share the research output of a university. The Bodleian was a forerunner in setting up a system for Oxford University, known as ORA (Oxford University Research Archive), which ensures that all research papers published by University staff and students are made available online for free, in a huge step for the concept of open access. Book chapters, journal articles, theses and conference papers must all be added to the institutional repository within three months of publication. Some key statistics about ORA are laid out below:

Number of complete works held in ORA available to the public	15,685
Number of complete works added 2014/15	8,554

FASCICULING

Protecting single-sheet items in the collection has always proved something of a challenge. Letters, photographs, postcards, pamphlets, flyers and other ephemera have often been especially difficult to store and in the past have been bundled up in boxes or bound together into a guardbook. Both these methods can lead to the damage of individual items as by their very nature they are not regular in size and so edges can become frayed and sheets puckered or torn. As a result, in 1981 book conservator Christopher Clarkson invented a new system which he called 'fasciculing', unique to the Bodleian, to house single-sheet items in the collection in such a way as to protect them and make them easy to shelve and consult. The system uses 120 gsm paper to create 15-leaf booklets with an acid-free stiff paper cover. Each loose item can then be attached into the fascicule using thin strips of Japanese RK17 paper. By pasting these to the extreme edge of the item a double-sided letter may be secured into the fascicule but is still able to be consulted on both sides. The reader then turns the pages of the fascicule rather than needing to touch the items themselves. One or two items per page are pasted into the fascicule, meaning that each fascicule holds a maximum of 30 items; five or ten fascicules in the standard 'c' size (see p. 70) fit together in an archival box, which can then be shelved. In the last decade (2005 to 2015) the number of fascicules created per year were:

YEAR	ITEMS	FASCICULES
2005/06	13,668	1,275
2006/07	24,447	1,055
2007/08	22,926	763
2008/09	22,928	816
2009/10	25,983	957
2010/11	31,281	1,073
2011/12	25,211	853
2012/13	21,538	764
2013/14	16,576	464
2014/15	6,008	285

Average number of items pasted each year   21,056
    into a fascicule

Average number of fascicules made each year   830

EARLY BOOK CONSERVATION

In 1673 a collection of 160 manuscripts collected by antiquarian and Yorkshire specialist Roger Dodsworth (1585–1654) was brought to the Bodleian after being bequeathed to the library by Thomas Fairfax. Unfortunately it was transported in torrential wet weather and the manuscripts were all affected by the damp. In what could be one of the earliest examples of book conservation at the Bodleian Library, antiquarian Anthony Wood rescued the soggy manuscripts by laying them out on the lead roof of the picture gallery, a process which took some weeks before all the manuscripts were satisfactorily dried.

BODLEIAN TREASURES:
THE GOUGH MAP

The Gough Map (MS. Gough. Gen. Top. 16) is one of the earliest maps to show Great Britain in a geographically recognizable form; it was likely created in the 1370s (though later revisions were made to it). It measures 56 × 115 cm. The map was drawn with pen and ink on parchment and shows 600 settlements, about 200 rivers and a curious network of red lines. It is not known who the map was created for, or why, but it lends scholars a valuable glimpse of Britain during the fourteenth century. The map is named after Richard Gough (see p. 43), a great collector, who purchased it in 1774 for the princely sum of half a crown. He later bequeathed his whole collection to the Bodleian.

THE GREAT GATES

The Great Gates of the Library open onto the Schools Quad; the coats of arms displayed upon the wooden gates tell the story of the foundation of the University. Starting from the top left are the arms of the University, followed by those of James I (indicating royal patronage) and then the Prince of Wales (later Charles I). There follow the coats of arms of the various colleges which made up the University in order of their foundation:

University College (1249) | Balliol (1263) | Merton (1264)
Exeter (1314) | Oriel (1326) | Queen's (1340)
New College (1379) | Lincoln (1427) | All Souls (1438)
Magdalen (1458) | Brasenose (1509) | Corpus Christi (1517)
Christ Church (1546) | Trinity (1555) | St John's (1555)
Jesus (1571) | Wadham (1610)

Pembroke College is not depicted as it was founded in 1624, after the gates had been made.

The *Staff Manual* from 1919 reveals the many and varied tasks assigned to the staff at the Bodleian. A small note indicates the impact of the First World War on the normal workings of the library: 'Owing to the absences of Assistants on military service a number of duties have been transferred to other members of the staff.' Below is a selection of the tasks the staff were expected to complete on a monthly basis:

Special monthly fire-alarm report

To be cleaned out:
1. Hot water channels in Bodley
2. Gutters on roof of Bodley
3. Gratings of Sheldonian basement windows

To be cleaned:
1. Floor and windows of Sheldonian basement
2. Floors of old Ashmolean basement
3. Quadrangle doors (and their locks oiled)

Wheeling-cases to be oiled:
1. Music-School
2. Law-room
3. Old Ashmolean basement (both rooms)

Clean lino in Music School

Camera basement to be cleaned

Underground bookstore to be cleaned

Camera drains to be flushed

Absence book to be made up

Register of loans and borrowings to be inspected

Cycle stands to be inspected

Contents of scrap drawer to be dealt with

Camera chimney and flue to be swept

Picture Gallery to be swept

Monthly accounts to be called in

THE GLADSTONE LINK

After the opening of the huge Book Storage Facility in Swindon in 2010, the librarians were able to move thousands of the least consulted books out of the underground storage at the Radcliffe Camera to Swindon. This allowed the opening up of the vast underground space between the Radcliffe Camera and the Old Bodleian, which since 1912 had been used for book storage. The new area is named after Victorian prime minister William Ewart Gladstone (1809–1898), who designed the original iron bookshelves which hung from rollers from the beams or roof frame.* It opens up for the first time a link for readers between the Radcliffe Camera and the Old Bodleian. The Gladstone Link now contains open-access books and greater reading space. Some key facts are given below:

Originally excavated	1909–12
Size of Gladstone Link	1,674 square metres†
Shelf space for	270,000 items
Reader spaces	120
Library catalogue code	BOD Gladstone

The Upper Level of the Gladstone Link houses a weekly new-book display and the continuation of the History Faculty Library's main lending collection, which begins in the Lower Camera. The Lower Level houses some recent Bodleian acquisitions in humanities; high-usage items, which are coded UBHU; humanities journals; the Slavonic History Reference Collection; and the Po Chung Personal Development Collection.

---

* A portion of these historic shelves, built in Jericho at Eagle Ironworks, have been preserved in the Gladstone Link for posterity. Gladstone jotted down the design for the shelves on the back on an envelope on a visit to the Bodleian in 1888 – this envelope is preserved in the Bodleian archives.

† In order that readers do not get lost in the Link, the lobbies connecting it to the libraries have been colour-coded: (b) for blue, for Bodleian; and (r) for red, for Radcliffe Camera. Should any students become disorientated and go astray there is also a coloured pathway connecting the two lobbies, pale blue on the main level and pale red in the basement.

THE 12 MILLIONTH BOOK

In November 2015 the Bodleian Library announced it had acquired its 12 millionth book, a revolutionary poem long thought lost entitled *Poetical Essay on the Existing State of Things* by Percy Bysshe Shelley. Published in 1811, the work is thought to have been written by Shelley during his two terms at the University of Oxford in 1810/11. Shelley originally published the poem, written as a response to Britain's involvement in the Napoleonic Wars, under a pseudonym, 'A Gentleman of the University of Oxford'. It was not confirmed by scholars as written by Shelley himself until fifty years after his death. The copy obtained by the Bodleian is considered to be the only one to have survived and was thought lost until it showed up in a private collection in 2006. Of great interest to Shelley scholars and fans alike, the poem reveals the young Shelley's political passions and belief that change can be fomented through poetry. The Bodleian has long been a leading repository of Shelley's works and papers, and this rare poem is now made available online to all who wish to enjoy it.

BODLEIAN TREASURES:
VERNON MANUSCRIPT

The Vernon manuscript (MS. Eng. poet. a. 1) is a late-fourteenth-century book, named after its donor Colonel Edward Vernon. It is the largest surviving anthology of Middle English literature. The huge, beautifully decorated manuscript, which weighs over 22 kg, was gifted to the library in 1677. One of the most important English books of the medieval period to have survived, it is a collection of poetry and prose comprising some 370 texts – each one on a moral or religious subject, reflecting the beliefs of the medieval Church. Written in a West Midlands dialect, it is a treasure trove for scholars of the English language.

EXHIBITIONS AND ENGAGEMENT

Since 1968, when the Bodleian took over the running of the Divinity School and Proscholium as exhibition spaces, the Bodleian has every year held a number of exhibitions inspired by the collection. Statistics on the exhibitions at the Bodleian from 2014/15 are given below:

Number of visitors to physical exhibitions	186,603
Number of visitors to online exhibitions	86,780
Number of visitors to the Divinity School	60,974
Number of visitors taking audio tours	4,943
Number of visitors taking guided tours	115,366

The top five most popular exhibitions to date have been:

EXHIBITION	YEAR	VISITORS
Marks of Genius	2015	164,355
Magical Books	2013	104,161
Charles Dickens and His World	2012	59,687
Beyond the Work of One: Oxford College Libraries and Their Benefactors	2008	58,024
John Aubrey: My Wit Was Always Working	2010	45,460

COLOUR-CODING BOOKS

In the mid-nineteenth century the twelfth Bodley's Librarian Henry Coxe attempted to reorganize the somewhat chaotic classification system in the Library by using colours to classify books in the collection by subject. The idea was that by applying a sticker with the correct subject colour to a book it could remain in its current location but the subject could be identified at a glance. Coxe planned that unbound books could be bound in the correct colour code and those already bound would have coloured stickers applied. The colour/subject code created by Coxe was as follows:

Purple	Theology
Yellow	Medicine
Brown	Arts and Trades
Chocolate	Law
Green	Maths and Physics
Pink	History
Blue	Poetry and Literature
Lavender	Classics
Red	Philology

Unfortunately this scheme proved to be too complex and was soon dropped. Some colour labels survive today on books in the library, but unfortunately over time they have become so faded that the colours have become indistinguishable from one another.

HEATING (OR LACK THEREOF) IN THE LIBRARY

The hazards of working in a freezing cold, unheated library in the depths of winter were acknowledged by many Oxford academics. George Hickes, a scholar of Anglo-Saxon, wrote in 1696 of the awful effects of the cold, ascribing to the long hours working in the Bodleian the death of both Gerard Langbaine (1609–1658), Provost of The Queen's College and Keeper of the University Archives, and orientalist Samuel Clarke (1625–1669).

In 1821 attempts were made to address the problem of the lack of heating in the Library. A stove was installed, at a safe distance outside the Library (to adhere to the no 'fire or flame' rule), which introduced warm air into the Arts End via two small vents. The system was fairly ineffectual and it was said that the librarians were apt to gather round the vents in the vain hope of getting warm.

In 1845 the Library finally got some proper means of heating, when steam pipes were fitted along the walls of Duke

Humfrey's Library below the windows. This system went some way to improving conditions, but it still got very cold in the winter months. One student, Friedrich Max Müller, wrote of the freezing conditions in his autobiography, describing the Bodleian as a 'Siberian library'. Luckily for him the kindly sub-librarian Mr Coxe* took pity on the freezing student and let him borrow a Russian fur coat to keep out the chill.

In 1856, due to concerns over the fire risk presented by the old wooden library, the heating system was turned off; in 1857 the pipes were insulated in slate to keep them from touching the highly flammable wooden floors so the system could be used once more.

Some of the problems with the Bodleian, such as lack of heating and short opening hours due to lack of lighting, were solved in 1862 when the Radcliffe Camera was incorporated into the Bodleian as a new reading room. The Camera had gas lighting and thus was open to students for twelve hours a day.

COLOURS FOR BINDING
FIFTEENTH-CENTURY BOOKS

Book binding has always been a necessary skill in the Library. The 1929 *Staff Manual* reveals the colours of the bindings used for fifteenth-century books according to which country the book was printed in:

COUNTRY	COLOUR
Germany & North Switzerland	black
France & Geneva	blue
Italy	brown
Spain and Portugal	orange
Holland & Belgium	green
England	maroon

---

* Twelfth Bodley's Librarian Henry Coxe kept a close eye on the dipping temperatures and often noted them down in his diary; for example, he noted that in January 1841 it was frequently at freezing point.

FETCHING BOOKS IN 1926

The *Staff Manual* of 1926 contains elaborate instructions on how books were to be transported using the underground link connecting the Radcliffe Camera and the Old Library which had opened in 1912. Boys were employed to fetch the books using a trolley and a man operated the lift. The first trolley went at 9 a.m. Thereafter:

Between 9.30 and 12.45 the trolley will go backwards and forwards between Bodley and the Camera, starting from Bodley at each half-hour, the trolley worker going on each journey end to end.

After the 12.30 p.m. lift, the service (starting at Bodley) will be as follows:

1. From Bodley to Camera
    (a) All books for Camera readers
    (b) All books to be replaced at Cam.
    (c) All non-urgent order for Bodl. books by Cam. readers
    (d) All non-urgent messages &c. for Camera

2. From Camera to Bodley
    (a) All Camera books for Bodley readers
    (b) All books to be replaced by Bodley
    (c) All non-urgent orders by Camera readers for Bodley books
    (d) All non-urgent messages &c. for Bodley.

The bells at the head and foot of the Lift are worked respectively by a Bodley boy and the man working the trolley. The code of signals is:–

STROKE	FROM BELOW	FROM ABOVE
ONE	'Lift going up'	'Lift received'
TWO	'Lift received'	'Lift going down'
THREE	'Let me speak to you'	

This tightly controlled system kept the books moving between the two libraries in an efficient manner. It is interesting to see 'new' technology starting to creep into the system – a note relating to urgent book orders reads: 'Orders for books urgently required, and special messages, may be telephoned. In the former case the original order-slip should be kept, and the duplicate made by the person receiving the telephone order should be marked "telephone order".'

THE CONVEYOR

During discussions about the design of the New Bodleian it was immediately clear that there needed to be some way of linking it with the existing Bodleian buildings in the Quad so that books could be easily transported between the two. The central section of the new building was a giant, eleven-storey bookstack which would house over 3.5 million books, and these needed to be accessible to people in the reading rooms of the Old Bodleian. To solve this a tunnel was excavated underneath Broad Street and the mechanical genius Sydney W. Rooke designed a 286.5-metre-long conveyor to carry boxes of books between the two. The conveyor rose upwards to the reading rooms on the Old Bodleian side from the bookstack on the other side, where it had a station on each floor of the eleven-storey bookstack. It was a masterpiece of engineering – it confounded and amazed in equal measure, moving at a rate of 0.3 metres per second or 0.67 mph. The conveyor was fundamental to the Library until it was finally turned off in 2010. By this time it had travelled approximately 74,477 miles, which is equivalent to 2.99 times the earth's circumference at the equator.

SANSKRIT

The Bodleian is home to the greatest collection of works in Sanskrit outside Asia. Accumulating the 8,700 manuscripts began back in the seventeenth century. The size and importance of the collection was significantly enhanced when, in 1827, Colonel Boden founded a Sanskrit chair – the only such professorship in Britain. This guaranteed the study of Sanskrit and encouraged both the donation and the acquisition of manuscripts and books in that language. A few items in the collection are extremely rare, including a fifth-century Buddhist work written on fifty strips of birch bark; another, written on palm leaf, is one of only three known to have survived from the Indian Buddhist monastic University of Nālandā. The Sanskrit collection was vastly increased and improved in 1909 when the prime minister of Nepal, Maharajah Sir Chandra Shum Shere, donated his collection of 6,000 manuscripts. The collection was further augmented when the Indian Institute and its library came under the control of the Bodleian in 1927. It continues to grow today, with around 2,000 printed Sanskrit books coming into the library each year.

THOMAS BODLEY IN HIS OWN WORDS

Reliquiæ Bodleianæ was published in 1703 and encompassed
Bodley's first statutes and a collection of his letters to Thomas
James. Edited by T. Hearne, the book includes a short autobiography written by Thomas Bodley himself in 1608. Bodley
wrote of his reasons for setting up the library:

> For thus I fell to discourse, and debate in my Mind,
> That altho' I might find it fittest for me, to keep out the
> Throng of Court Contentions, and address my Thoughts
> and Deeds to such Ends altogether, as I my self could
> best affect; yet withal I was to think, that my Duty
> towards God, the Expectation of the World, and my
> natural Inclination, and very Morality did require, that
> I should not wholly so hide those little Abilities that I
> had, but that in some measure, in one kind or other, I
> should do the true part of a profitable Member of the
> State; whereupon examining exactly for the rest of my
> life, what course I might take, and having sought (as I
> thought) all the ways to the Wood, to select the most
> proper, I concluded at the last, to set up my Staff at the
> Library-Door in Oxon; being thoroughly perswaded, that
> in my Solitude, and Surcease from the Common-Wealth
> Affairs, I could not busy my self to better purpose, than
> by reducing that Place (which then in every Part lay
> ruined and wast) to the publick use of Students.

BODLEIAN LIBRARY TIMELINE
OF KEY EVENTS

c. 1320   The first library for Oxford University (some
          individual colleges had libraries before)
          opened in the Old Congregation House, in
          the University Church, with the donation of a
          number of books from Thomas Cobham, the
          Bishop of Worcester

1424   Foundation stone laid for the Divinity School

c. 1455   Johannes Gutenberg printed the first book
          using movable type, the Gutenberg Bible

1478   Building started on Duke Humfrey's Library

1488   Duke Humfrey's Library opened, built to
          house his gift of 281 manuscripts

1550   Richard Cox, Dean of Christ Church, acting
          as part of the Royal Visitation under Edward
          VI to suppress 'Superstitious books', raided
          the Library and had most of the books burnt,
          destroyed or given away in an effort to purge
          the Library of Catholic texts

1556   With no funds to rebuild the book collection
          the library desks were sold and the building
          was given over to the Faculty of Medicine

1598   The University accepted Sir Thomas Bodley's
          gift of money to rebuild the library

1602   Thomas Bodley's library first opened to
          scholars with over 2,500 books; Thomas James
          appointed First Bodley's Librarian

1604   Bodley was knighted and the library was
          formally named the Bodleian Library

1605   The first printed catalogue was produced

1610   Bodley reached an agreement with the
          Stationers' Company of London that a copy
          of every book published in England would be
          deposited in the library

98

1610–12	As the collection grew, space was required so an extension, Arts End, was commissioned
1613	Thomas Bodley died
1613	Work started on the building of the Schools Quadrangle
1620	The first full catalogue to be alphabetized by author was produced
1620	First Librarian Thomas James resigned and was replaced by John Rouse
1634–40	A further extension to Duke Humfrey's Library, Selden End, was built
1635	Second Bodley's Librarian John Rouse published a supplement to the existing catalogue
1645	King Charles I was refused permission to borrow a book
1662	The Press Licensing Act reaffirmed the principle of the Stationers' Company depositing books in the Royal Library, and the libraries of Oxford and Cambridge
1674	Thomas Hyde's Catalogue of Printed Books published
1712–13	The Clarendon Building was built as HQ for Oxford University Press
1737	Building started on the Radcliffe Library
1738	A revised catalogue of printed books published in two volumes
1749	The Radcliffe Library opened
1814	A catalogue of the Gough Collection was published
1830	Major renovation of the Picture Gallery
1832	The first display cases were purchased to exhibit manuscripts in Arts End
1835	Radcliffe Library printed its first catalogue
1840	Catalogue of the Douce Collection published
1845	The Bodleian library got heating at last

1845	University Gallery (now Ashmolean Museum) opened
1856	Undergraduates were given access to the Library
1859	The University gave over the last of the ground-floor rooms in the quadrangle to the library, meaning that the whole of the Schools Quadrangle now belonged to the Bodleian (except for two rooms in the tower where the archives of the University were stored).
1861	The Radcliffe Library became part of the Bodleian and was renamed the Radcliffe Camera
1862	The Radcliffe Camera reopened as a reading room for the Bodleian
1897–1901	The Radcliffe Science Library was built on South Parks Road
1905	Electric lights were installed in the Radcliffe Camera
1907	The Picture Gallery was refurbished and reopened as the Upper Reading Room
1909–12	The bookstore underneath Radcliffe Square was excavated
1910	First woman member of permanent staff, Frances Underhill, was appointed
1914	The number of books in the Bodleian collection breached 1 million
1914	The first edition of the magazine *Bodleian Quarterly Record* was published
1919	First internal telephone system installed for Library staff
1919	Fifteenth Bodley's Librarian Arthur Cowley bought a typewriter for the Library
1925	Friends of the Bodleian was created
1925	The Law Faculty merged the Maitland Memorial Library of legal and social history into the Bodleian's law department library

1927	The Radcliffe Trustees established the Radcliffe Science Library as a dependent library under Bodleian management
1927	The Bodleian took over the running of the Indian Institute
1928	A lift was installed in the north stairwell
1929	Artificial lights were installed throughout the Library for the first time
1929	Rhodes House, devoted to the study of the Empire and the United States, became the third dependent Bodleian library
1937	HM Queen Mary laid the foundation stone of the New Bodleian
1937–40	The New Bodleian Library (now Weston Library) was built on Broad Street
1946	The New Library was officially opened by King George VI
1960–63	Duke Humfrey's Library underwent restoration, including resurfacing the facade in Clipsham stone
1964	New Law Library built on Manor Road
1967	A libraries board to coordinate the University libraries was established
1968	An extension was built atop the New Bodleian to house the Indian Institute Library
1968	The Bodleian took over running of the Divinity School and Proscholium as exhibition spaces
1974	New book storage space erected in Nuneham Courtenay
1975	New office space acquired for the Bodleian in the Clarendon Building, which resides in the space between the old and new libraries, and thus the historic core of the university came under Bodleian control
1975	Underground extension of Radcliffe Science Library completed

1988	Online cataloguing of books to national and international standards began
1994	A catalogue of all the pre-1920 books in the library became available on CD-ROM
2000	The Bodleian became the largest library in the newly formed Oxford University Library Services (OULS)
2002	The Bodleian celebrated its quatercentenary
2010	A new Book Storage Facility was opened just outside Swindon
2010	OULS was renamed Bodleian Libraries
2011	The underground bookstore, the Gladstone Link, at the Radcliffe Camera was opened to readers
2014	The remodelling of the New Bodleian by Wilkinson Eyre Architects was completed and the library was renamed the Weston Library
2015	The Library acquired its 12 millionth book

FURTHER READING

BOOKS

Aylmer, Ursula (ed.), *Most Noble Bodley, A Bodleian Library Anthology*, Oxford, 2002.

Bodleian Library (ed.), *Wonderful Things from 400 Years of Collecting: The Bodleian Library, 1602–2002*, Oxford, 2002.

Bodley, Sir Thomas, *The Life of Sir Thomas Bodley written by himself together with the first draft of the Statutes of the Public library at Oxon*, Chicago, 1906.

Clapinson, Mary, *A Brief History of the Bodleian Library*, Oxford, 2015.

Clarke, Andrew (ed.), *The Life and Times of Anthony Wood, 1632-1695, described by Himself*, Volume II: 1664–1681, Oxford, 1892; Volume III: 1682–1695, Oxford, 1894.

Clennell, William (ed.), *The Autobiography of Sir Thomas Bodley*, Oxford, 2006.

Craster, Edmund, *History of the Bodleian Library, 1845–1945*, Oxford, 1952.

Gillam, Stanley, *The Divinity School and Duke Humfrey's Library at Oxford*, Oxford, 1998.

Hampshire, Gwen (ed.), *The Bodleian Library Account Book 1613–1646*, Oxford, 1983.

Heaney, Michael, and Catríona Cannon (eds), *Transforming the Bodleian*, Oxford, 2012.

Holland, Robert W. (ed.), *Adversis Major: A Short History of the Educational Books Scheme of the Prisoners of War Department of the British Red Cross Society and Order of St. John of Jerusalem*, London, 1949.

Hebron, Stephen, *Marks of Genius*, Oxford, 2015.

Hebron, Stephen, *Dr Radcliffe's Library*, Oxford, 2015.

Norris, John, *A Catalogue of Pictures, Models, Busts &c. In the Bodleian Gallery, Oxford*, Oxford, 1839.

Macray, William Dunn, *Annals of the Bodleian Library*, Oxford, 1890.

Philip, Ian G. *The Bodleian Library in the Seventeenth and Eighteenth Centuries: Lyell Lectures 1980–1981*, Oxford, 1983.

Rogers, David, *The Bodleian Library and its Treasures, 1320–1700*, Oxford, 1991.

Spedding, James, Robert Leslie Ellis and Douglas Denon Heath, *The Works of Francis Bacon, Volume 3: The Letters and the Life*, London, 1868.

Tickell, Thomas, *Oxford, a poem*, Oxford, 1707.

Tyack, Geoffrey, *Bodleian Library Souvenir Guide*, Oxford, 2000 (rev. 2014).

Vaisey, David, *Bodleian Library Treasures*, Oxford, 2015.

Wheeler, G.W. (ed.), *Letters of Sir Thomas Bodley to the University of Oxford*, Oxford, 1927.

Wheeler, G.W. (ed.), *Letters of Sir Thomas Bodley to Thomas James*, Oxford, 1926.

ARTICLES

Clapinson, Mary, 'Henry Octavius Coxe 1811–1881', Dictionary of National Biography, Oxford, 2004.

Clapinson, Mary, 'Edward Williams Byron Nicholson 1849–1912', Dictionary of National Biography, Oxford, 2004.

Clennell, William H., 'Sir Thomas Bodley 1545–1613', Dictionary of National Biography, Oxford, 2004.

Clennell, William H. 'The Bodleian Declaration: A History', Bodleian Library Record 20, 2007, pp. 47–60.

Moran, Barbara B., 'E.W.B. Nicholson and the Hiring of the First Woman at the Bodleian Library', Bodleian Library Record, vol. 25, no. 2, October 2012, pp. 284–96.

Smith, L. Herman, 'Manuscript Repair in European Archives', The American Archivist, vol. 1, no. 1, 1938, pp. 1–22.

Williams, Abigail, 'Ragtime to Riches: The Remarkable Story of Walter Harding's Collection', Bodleian Library Record, vol. 25, no. 2, 2012, pp. 239–47.

Campaign Dinner, Bodleian Library Record, vol. 13, 1988–1991, p. 95.

PRIMARY SOURCES

Bodleian Staff Manual, Bodleian Library, Oxford, 1920, 1929, 1932, 1937.

Library Records d.1873.

Staff-Kalendar, Bodleian Library, Oxford, 1904.

Calendar of State Papers, domestic, 1598.

INDEX